YOUR MONEY

OR YOUR LIFE

Translated by Patricia Ranum

YOUR MONEY

OR YOUR LIFE

Economy and Religion in the Middle Ages

Jacques Le Goff

ZONE BOOKS · NEW YORK

1990

Printed in the United States of America

Originally published as *La Bourse et La Vie*
© 1986 Hachette
La Bourse et La Vie has appeared in the series *TEXTES DU XXe
SIECLE*, edited by Maurice Olender.

Quotations from Dante Alighieri, *The Divine Comedy*, Trans-
lated, with a Commentary, by Charles S. Singleton, Bollingen
Series LXXX, Vol. 1, *Inferno*. Copyright © 1970 by Princeton
University Press. Reprinted by permission.

Quotations from Ezra Pound, *The Cantos of Ezra Pound*. Copyright © 1934, 1948 by Ezra Pound. Reprinted by permission of
New Directions Publishing Company.

Distributed by The MIT Press
Cambridge, Massachusetts, and London, England

Library of Congress Cataloging in Publication Data

Le Goff, Jacques, 1924-
    Your money or your life.

    Translation of: La bourse et la vie.
    Bibliography: p.
1. Economic history—Medieval, 500-1500.
2. Church history — Middle Ages, 600-1500.
I. Title.
HC41.L43 1988   330.94'01   87-25248
ISBN 0-942299-14-0 (alk. paper)
ISBN 0-942299-15-9 (pbk.)

To the memory of Robert S. Lopez

Contents

Chapter I

Between the Devil and Mammon:

Usury and the Usurer

Usury. For seven hundred years, from the twelfth through the nineteenth century, what phenomenon in the Western world presented such an explosive mixture of economics and religion, money and salvation? The word conjures up the image of a long Middle Ages in which a new type of man was crushed beneath the weight of ancient symbols, in which modernity painfully elbowed its way through sacred taboos, and in which the cunning of history used the repressive forces of religious power as the tools for earthly success.

The great controversy surrounding usury constitutes what might be called the "labor pains of capitalism." Anyone who hears the term *usury* and thinks of the pawnbroker as that residuum, that ghost of the usurer as he is portrayed in nineteenth-century English novels, and in Hollywood films made after the Great Depression of 1929, can understand neither his role as a protagonist of Western society – who hovers like a monstrous shadow over the progress of the monetary economy – nor the social and ideological stakes that coalesced around this precapitalist Dracula. The usurer was a doubly frightening vampire for Christian society, because this money-hungry creature was often likened to the Jew, that deicide, that infanticide, that profaner of the sacred host. His was a world where money (*nummus* in Latin, *denier* in French) was "God"[1] and where, as the saying goes, "Money conquers, money reigns, money is sovereign" (*Nummus vincit, nummus regnat, nummus imperat*).[2] It was a world where *avaritia*, or cupidity, a bourgeois sin that was more or less the mother of usury, had usurped the throne of the chief of the Seven Deadly Sins, *superbia*, or pride, a feudal sin. For that world, the usurer, a specialist in lending money at interest, became a necessary but detested man, powerful but also vulnerable.

Usury was one of the major issues of the thirteenth century. At that time, Christianity, at the apogee of the vigorous growth it had been achieving since the year 1000, was already in jeopardy. The sudden eruption and spread of the monetary economy threatened old Christian values. Capitalism, a new economic system, was ready to take shape. If it did not require new technology to get started, it at least made wholesale use of practices that had always been condemned by the Church. The fierce daily struggle, which took place at the junction between values and ways of thinking (*mentalités*), was marked by repeated interdictions. At stake was the legitimation of lawful profit, which had to be differentiated from unlawful usury.

Christianity traditionally placed God in opposition to money. How could it vindicate wealth, or at any rate ill-acquired wealth? Ecclesiastes 31:5 states: "The lover of gold will not be free from sin, for he who pursues wealth is led astray by it."

And the gospel echoed this text. Matthew, a publican, a tax collector who abandoned his silver-laden table in order to follow Jesus, warned: "No man can serve two masters; for either he will hate the one and love the other, or else he will stand by the one and despise the other. You cannot serve God and Mammon" (Matt. 6:24). In late rabbinical literature, Mammon symbolized iniquitous wealth, money. Luke 16:13 used virtually the same words to express the same position.

Although codes, laws, precepts, and decrees condemned usury, God was solely interested in men — like the historian who, as Marc Bloch used to put it, "hunted" men. Let us therefore go hunting for usurers. To find them, we must not restrict ourselves to official documents. Ecclesiastical and lay legislation was primarily interested in usury, while religious practice focused on the usurers themselves. Evidence regarding thirteenth-century practice is found in two types of documents derived from older genres that underwent a fundamental mutation during the late twelfth and early thirteenth century. The first documents are the *summae*, or confessors' manuals. During the early Middle Ages, a list of penances, which varied according to the nature of the sinful act, was recorded in *penitentials*. Modeled after the laws of the barbarians, these manuals focused upon the acts, not upon the actors. Or rather, the categories to which the actors belonged were judicial ones: clergy or laymen, free men or not free.

But between the late eleventh century and the early thirteenth century, the concept of sin and penance changed profoundly, became spiritualized and internalized. The gravity of a sin was henceforth measured in terms of the sinner's intention. It was therefore necessary to determine whether this intention was good or bad. This morality of intention was taught in every major twelfth-century theological school, from Laon to St. Victor of Paris, from Chartres to Notre Dame; and despite their disagreements on many other issues, it was professed by all the leading theologians, Abelard and St. Bernard, Gilbert de la Porrée and Peter Lombard, Peter Cantor and Alan of Lille. As a result, a profound change occurred in the way confession was conducted. Previously a relatively unusual collective and public event reserved for the most serious sins, confession became auricular, transmitted from mouth to ear. It was transformed into an individual and private act that was widespread and frequent. The Fourth Lateran Council of 1215 was a landmark. It made confession obligatory for every man and woman at least once a year at Easter. The penitent was expected to comment on the sin as it related to his familial, social and professional situation, and explain the circumstances and motives involved. The confessor had to keep these individual parameters in mind and show as much concern, if not more, for soliciting the sinner's *confession* and for obtaining his *contrition*, as he did for "satisfaction," that is, for penance. His priority was to cleanse a person rather than chastise a fault.

This required the two partners in confession to make a great effort, one for which the past had not prepared them. The penitent had to question himself about his conduct and his intentions, he had to examine his conscience. A whole new frontier, introspection, had been created, and would slowly transform ways of thinking and behaving. These were the beginnings of psychological modernity. The confessor had to ask appropriate questions, so that he would become acquainted with his penitent and so that he could distinguish the grave sins, which are mortal if there is not contrition or penance, from the less serious ones, the venial sins for which one can atone. Sinners dying in a state of mortal sin will go to Hell, the traditional site of death and eternal punishment. The dead who are burdened solely by venial sins will spend more or less time expiating them in a new place, Purgatory, which they will leave, purified and purged, for the eternal life of Paradise, possibly having waited until the Last Judgment.

In these new penitential proceedings, what happened to the usurer? The confessors, confronted by a novel situation, by the often unfamiliar procedures of confession, and by embarrassing admissions or questions, needed guides, for they were hesitant about the nature of the interrogation that they were expected to conduct and about the penance to impose. Theologians, and above all canonists, wrote summaries and manuals for confessors. In some instances, these were learned and detailed treatises intended for educated confessors holding high rank in the Church; in others, they were quite brief guides for the humbler and less educated priests. But no one escaped scrutiny, and usury has its place in all these reference books. The usurer is discussed less often, for weighing his position involved a certain amount of personalized evaluation that was left to the confessor's judgment.

The usurer was, on the other hand, the principal protagonist in the second type of document, the *exempla*. An *exemplum* is a brief narrative, presented as true and intended for use in a speech, generally a sermon, in order to convince an audience by means of a salutary lesson. The story is brief, easy to remember, and convincing. It uses rhetoric and narrative effects, and it seizes the imagination. Amusing or, more often, terrifying, it dramatizes. The preacher is offering a little talisman that, if one is willing to grasp its message and make use of it, should bring salvation. He is offering a key to Heaven.

Here is one of the numerous *exempla* about usurers, taken from Jacques de Vitry, who died shortly before 1240.

Another very rich usurer was beginning to struggle against the pangs of death, to lament, to suffer, and to implore his soul not to leave him, for he had satisfied its every whim; and he promised it gold and silver and the delights of this world, if only it would remain with him. But it must not ask him for the tiniest coin or for the smallest alms for the poor. Realizing at last that he could not hold onto his soul, he became angry and said to it indignantly: 'I have prepared for you a fine residence, with abundant wealth, but it has made you so crazy and so wretched that you do not want to dwell in this fine mansion. Go away! I commend you to all the devils of Hell.' Soon afterwards he surrendered his spirit into the hands of the demons and was buried in Hell.[3]

This was merely an outline. The preacher embroidered upon the theme. He used his voice and its intonations, he gesticulated. The subject itself was already impressive enough. It must have been heard by millions of listeners. For, in the Middle Ages, the sermon was a powerful medium which, in principle, reached all the faithful. We know, of course, thanks mainly to an *exemplum* about King Louis IX of France (better known as St. Louis) that men sometimes left the church during the sermon and went to its great rival, the tavern, a permanent temptation located just across the way. Whenever he witnessed this, St. Louis, scandalized, would have the stray parishioners brought back to hear the gospel. The thirteenth century also witnessed a great rebirth of preaching. Confronted by heretics, in particular the Cathari, and by a changing world that offered Christians an increasing number of earthly delights, the Church used the weapon of speech. To a society in transition, it addressed a message that was often innovative and that dealt with everyday life. Newly created religious orders stressed the spiritual value of poverty, as opposed to increasing one's wealth. Two of the

14

most important mendicant orders, the Franciscans and the Dominicans (the latter forming the Order of the Friars Preachers), specialized in preaching. Having preached the crusade, they now preached reform, and called upon stars who would attract crowds. Although a layman, Jacques de Vitry was one of these stars; still preoccupied with the crusade, he preached primarily of the new society. His model sermons, with their outlined *exempla*, were widely reproduced and disseminated, even after the thirteenth century. And Vitry's story of the usurer, which may have been a highly popular anecdote, evokes the most agonizing moment in a Christian's existence, his death pangs. Its action focuses upon the duality of man: his soul and his body. It portrays the great social antagonism between the rich and poor and between gold and silver, those new protagonists of human existence. And it finishes with the worst possible way to end a life: the madman's summoning of demons, the evocation of devils whose hands inflict torture, and the burial of the damned both below the ground and beyond the grave. Refused burial in hallowed ground, the cadaver of the impenitent usurer was immediately buried, forever, in Hell. Salvation comes to him who gets the message! "Usurers! This will be your fate." These anecdotes, which were spoken, heard, and circulated, provide the key source for our investigation of the usurer during the Middle Ages.

Usury is a sin. Why? What curse lies upon the usurer's money pouch, which he cherishes, which he is no more willing to part with than Molière's miser, Harpagon, was willing to part with his money box, and that sends him to eternal death? To save himself, must he forsake his pouch? Or will he find — or will someone find for him — a way to hang onto both his money *and* his life, his eternal life? This is the usurer's great struggle, a struggle between wealth and Heaven, between money and Hell.

CHAPTER II

The Moneybag: Usury

Today we speak of *usury* in the singular. Medieval men and their texts also sometimes used the singular, *usura*. But usury has many faces. Thirteenth-century acts usually use the plural form: *usurae*. Usury is a many-headed monster, a hydra. Jacques de Vitry devotes the third paragraph of his model sermon 59, *De multiplici usura*, to an evocation of this multiform usury. Likewise, in his *Summa confessorum*, Thomas of Chobham first defines "usury in general" and then, in Chapter IV, *De variis casibus*, describes its "different cases" before finally returning, in Chapter X, to "other cases of usury." The word *usury* denotes a multiplicity of practices, thus complicating any distinction between the lawful and the unlawful in transactions involving interest. This difficult but necessary distinction between usury and interest, this horrible fascination with a multiform beast, was never better appreciated than by the twentieth-century poet, Ezra Pound:

> *The Evil is Usury,* neschek
> *the serpent*
> neschek *whose name is known, the defiler,*
> *beyond race and against race*

the defiler
Τόχος hic mali medium est
Here is the core of evil, the burning hell without let-up,
The canker corrupting all things, Fafnir the worm,
Syphilis of the State, of all kingdoms,
Wart of the commonweal,
Wenn-maker, corrupter of all things.
Darkness the defiler,
Twin evil of envy,
Snake of the seven heads, Hydra, entering all things...[1]

But there is also *usura*, usury per se, the common denominator in a group of forbidden financial practices. Usury means that a lender receives interest through transactions that should not produce interest. And so, usury is not the levying of *all* interest. Usury and interest are not synonymous, nor are usury and profit. Usury is involved where there is no production or physical transformation of tangible goods.

Thomas of Chobham begins his exposé on usury with these thoughts: "In all other contracts, I can expect and receive a profit [*lucrum*], just as, when I have given you something, I can expect a counter-gift [*antidotum*], that is to say, a reply to the gift [*contra datum*]; and I can hope to *receive*, since I gave to you first. Likewise, if I loan you my clothes or my furniture, I can receive something in return. Why is this not also the case if I have loaned you my money [*denarios meos*]?"[2]

Here is the issue in a nutshell: the status of *money* in medieval ecclesiastical doctrine and thought is the basis for the condemnation of usury. This is not the place for a strictly economic study, which would have to take into account the way in which people of the time received the realities that we today isolate within a specific category called economics. Their perception was very different from ours.

The only modern historian and theorist of the economy who can help us understand the functioning of "economics" in medieval society is, to my mind, Karl Polanyi (1886–1964). To avoid all anachronisms, we must keep in mind two observations made by Polanyi and his collaborators, if we wish to attempt an analysis of the medieval phenomenon of usury within an economic perspective. The first observation, borrowed from Malinowski, concerns the gift and the counter-gift.

> In the group of transactions, where the gift is expected to be returned in an economically equivalent manner, we meet another confusing fact. This is the category which according to our notions ought to be practically indistinguishable from trade. Far from it. Occasionally the identically same object is exchanged back and forth between the partners, thus depriving the transaction of any conceivable economic purpose or meaning! By the simple device of handing back, though in a roundabout way, the pig to its donor, the exchange of equivalencies instead of being a step in the direction of economic rationality proves a safeguard against the intrusion of utilitarian considerations. The sole purpose of the exchange is to draw relationships closer by strengthening the ties of reciprocity.[3]

Granted, the economy of the thirteenth-century West is not the economy of the natives of the Trobriand Islands during the early twentieth century; but, though it is more complex, the notion of *reciprocity* nonetheless dominates the theory of economic exchanges in a society founded upon "a network of relations" that are Christian and feudal.

19

Polanyi's second usable concept involves *embedding* and *institutional analysis*.

> We must rid ourselves of the ingrained notion that the economy is a field of experience of which human beings have necessarily always been conscious. To use a metaphor, the facts of the economy were originally embedded in situations that were not in themselves of an economic nature, neither the ends nor the means being primarily material. The crystallization of the concept of the economy was a matter of time and history. But neither time nor history have provided us with those conceptual tools required to penetrate the maze of social relationships in which the economy is embedded. This is a task of what we will call institutional analysis.[4]

To which I would like to add cultural and psychological analysis. This essay aims to show men, usurers, within the aggregate of social relations, practices, and values in which the economic phenomenon of usury is embedded. In other words, my analysis will be linked to usury as a whole, as it is reflected in the behavior and in the image of the usurer, who practiced usury.

When confronted by a phenomenon, medieval men would seek its model in the Bible. Biblical authority supplied at once the origin, the explanation, and the application of the issue in question. If the medieval Church and medieval society were not paralyzed by biblical authority and not forced into historical immobility, it was because the Bible often contradicted itself (*sic et non*, yes and no) and because, as Alan of Lille wrote at the end of the twelfth century, "authorities have a waxen nose," they can be shaped at will by exegetes and readers.

But when it came to the condemnation of usury, there

seemed to be scarcely any disagreement or rift. The scriptural file on usury includes essentially five texts, four of which are in the Old Testament.

1. "If you lend money to one of your poor neighbors among my people, you shall not act like an extortioner to him by demanding interest from him." (Exod. 22:24)

This interdiction, which was obeyed by the Jewish community, was also respected by medieval Christians, aware that they formed a fraternity in which the *poor*, above all, had special rights. The revival of the value of poverty during the thirteenth century would further heighten indignation about the Christian usurer.

2. "When one of your fellow countrymen is reduced to poverty and is unable to hold out beside you, extend to him the privileges of an alien or a tenant, so that he may continue to live with you. Do not exact interest from your countrymen either in money or in kind, but out of fear of God let him live with you." (Lev. 25:35–37)

This text was particularly important because of its Latin rendering in the Vulgate of St. Jerome, the authoritative text of the Middle Ages. The final sentence read, "*Pecuniam tuam non dabis ei ad usuram et frugum superabundatiam non exiges*" — literally, "You will not give him your money upon usury and you will not exact a superabundance of victuals." Two expressions, culled by Christians, retained their effectiveness throughout the Middle Ages: *ad usuram*, "upon usury," which clearly forbade usury; and *superabundantia*, "superabundance," the "surplus," which censured excess.

3. "You shall not demand interest from your countrymen on a loan of money or of food or of anything else on which interest is usually demanded. You may demand interest from a

foreigner, but not from your countrymen." (Deut. 23:20–21)

In the expression "*non foenerabis fratri tuo*," note the Vulgate's use of a word borrowed from Roman law: *fenerare*, "to lend for interest," "to carry on usury," an expression that favored the creation during the twelfth century of Romano-canonical legislation against usury. During the Middle Ages, the authorization to carry on usury with foreigners functioned in the direction Jew to Christian, but not in the opposite direction since medieval Christians did not view Jews as foreigners. On the other hand, they likened their enemies to foreigners and, in the event of war, considered usury lawful if it would harm the adversary. Gratian's *Decretum* of circa 1140, the die from which Canon Law was cast, employed St. Ambrose's formula: "*Ubi ius belli, ibi ius usurae*," that is, "Wherever there is the law of war, there is the law of usury."

4. According to Psalm 15, the usurer cannot be Jehovah's guest: "O Lord, who shall sojourn in your tent? Who shall dwell on your holy mountain? He who walks blamelessly, . . . who lends not his money at usury." The medieval Christian interpreted this psalm as barring the usurer from Heaven.

To these four texts can be added another Old Testament passage, this time from Ezekiel 18:13, which includes, among the violent and bloodthirsty people who arouse Jehovah's anger, anyone who "lends at interest and exacts usury." In this same passage, the prophet warns, "He shall surely die; his death shall be his own fault."

5. Lastly, in the New Testament, the gospel of Luke retained the Old Testament condemnation and expanded it, thus establishing the formal echo that medieval Christians expected of an authoritative scriptural passage. "If you lend to those from whom you expect repayment, what merit is there in it for you? Even

sinners lend to sinners, expecting to be repaid in full. Love your enemy and do good; lend, without expecting to be repaid in full." (Luke 6:34–35) What counted most in the Middle Ages were Luke's final words, "*Mutuum date, nihil inde sperantes*," because the idea of lending without hoping to be repaid was expressed by two key terms in medieval economic practice and thought. One was *mutuum*, a word borrowed from Roman law and designating a contract that transfers ownership and consists of a loan that must cost nothing. The other term was *sperare*, "to hope for," which in the Middle Ages referred to the self-interested hope of all economic actors engaged in a transaction that involved *time*, in other words, that stipulated a remunerated *wait* in return for profit (or loss) or for interest, be it lawful or unlawful.

A long Christian tradition also condemned usury. Early on, the Church Fathers expressed their scorn for usurers. The canons of the first councils forbade usury to clerics (canon 20 of the Council of Elivra, circa 300; and canon 17 of the Council of Nicaea, in 325), and then expanded the interdiction to laymen (the Council of Clichy, in 626). Charlemagne, above all, legislating in matters spiritual and temporal, forbade usury by clerics and laymen in his *Admonitio generalis* of Aix-la-Chapelle, dated 789. Usury thus had acquired a substantial record of condemnation by both ecclesiastical and lay powers. But usury was a secondary concern in a contracted economy where few coins were used and circulated. Indeed, monasteries supplied most of the necessary credit until the twelfth century. At the end of that century, the pope forbade them their preferred form of credit, the *mort-gage*, a "loan having as its collateral a building from which the money-lender receives the income."[5]

When the money economy became more widespread during the twelfth century, and when the wheel of fortune turned faster for knights and for noblemen, as well as for the burghers of the cities buzzing with work and business and throwing off their old fetters, then Lady Usury became an important personage. The Church grew alarmed. Nascent canon law and, shortly afterward, scholasticisim – which tried to conceive of and to prescribe the relationship between the new society and God – sought to stem this growing usury. If I recite the litany of the principal measures taken by church councils and the most important texts, it is simply to show the spread and the strength of the phenomenon, and the stubbornness with which the Church fought it. Each council – the Second Lateran Council of 1139, the Third Lateran Council of 1179, the Fourth Lateran Council of 1215, the Second Council of Lyon of 1274, and the Council of Vienna in 1311 – added a building block to the wall the Church was building to contain the wave of usury. The Code of Canon Law was also enriched by legislation against usury. In his *Decretum* of circa 1140, Gratian assembled twenty-nine scriptural and patristic "authorities." Urban III's decretal *Consuluit* of 1187 would take its place in the Code during the second quarter of the thirteenth century, beside the *Decretals* of Gregory IX. Theologians did not lag behind. Peter Lombard, the bishop of Paris who died in 1160, borrowed from St. Anselm for his *Sententiarum*, which became the textbook for thirteenth-century theology students. At the turn of the eleventh to twelfth century, St. Anselm had been the first to liken usury to theft, the first to place usury, a form of plunder, among those practices forbidden by the Fourth Commandment: "Thou shalt not steal" (*Non furtum facies*). Cardinal Robert of Courçon, canon of Noyon – who had lived in Paris since 1195, who led the Albigensian crusade in 1214, and who gave the young University of Paris its first statutes in 1215 – inserted a veritable treatise on

24

usury into his *Summa*, written prior to the Council of Paris of 1213, where he saw to it that stern measures would be taken against usurers. Holding usury and heresy to be the great evils of his day, he proposed that the plague of usury be combated by a vast offensive to be worked out by an ecumenical council. He viewed the usurer — and I shall return to this point — as universally slothful; and for Courçon sloth was the mother of all vices. The council, presided over by the pope and attended by all the bishops and princes, would order each Christian, under pain of excommunication and censure, to work either spiritually or physically and to earn his bread by the sweat of his brow, as St. Paul had taught. "And thus," Courçon concluded, "all usurers, all rebels and all plunderers would disappear, we would be able to give alms and provide for the churches, and everything would return to its original state."[6] After this portrayal of a utopia free of usury, all the great scholastics would devote a greater or lesser part of their *summae* to usury. This is the case with William of Auxerre, the bishop of Paris who died in 1248,[7] and for St. Bonaventure and St. Thomas Aquinas,[8] both of whom died in 1274. And then Giles of Lessines, Aquinas's disciple, wrote *De usuris*, a complete treatise on usury, between 1276 and 1285.

Between the mid-twelfth and the mid-thirteenth century, this growing censure of usury can be explained by the Church's fear that society would be disrupted by the proliferation of usurious practices. In 1179 the Third Lateran Council declared that too many men were abandoning their social station or their trade in order to become usurers. In the thirteenth century, Pope Innocent IV and the great canonist Hostiensis (also known as Henry of Segusio) expressed their fears that the countryside would be deserted, because peasants had become usurers or

had been deprived of their cattle and tools by landowners, themselves attracted by the profits of usury. The appeal of usury threatened to depopulate the countryside and hamper agriculture and
thus raised the specter of famine.

Medieval definitions of usury were based upon St. Ambrose:
"Usury is receiving more than one has given" *(Usura est plus accipere
quam dare)*;[9] upon St. Jerome: "One calls anything whatsoever
usury and surplus if one has collected more than one has given"
*(Usuram appellari et superabundantiam quidquid illus est, si ab eo quod
dederit plus acceperit)*;[10] upon the capitulary of Nijmwegen of 806:
"There is usury wherever one demands more than one gives"
(Usura est ubi amplius requiritur quam datur); and upon Gratian's
Decretum: "Everything that is demanded beyond the capital, is
usury" *(Quicquid ultra sortem exigitur usura est)*.[11] Usury is the unlawful surplus, the illegitimate excess.

Urban III's decretal *Consuluit* (1187), which was incorporated
into the Code of Canon Law, is undoubtedly the best expression of the Church's attitude toward usury during the thirteenth
century:

- Usury is everything that is asked in exchange for a loan,
  beyond the value of the loan itself;
- Earning money through usury is a sin forbidden by both the
  Old and the New Testaments;
- Merely hoping to receive additional property, beyond the
  property itself, is a sin;
- Total *restitution* of gain acquired through usury must be made
  to the true owner;
- Asking a higher price for a sale on credit is an implicit act
  of usury.

In the oldest known *Summa* for confessors, most of which
was drawn up before 1215 and probably put into circulation

26

before 1216, Thomas of Chobham uses the New Testament and Canon Law as his sole authorities on usury: "And the Lord said in the Gospel, 'Lend without expecting repayment' [Luke 6:35]. And Canon Law says, 'There is usury wherever one demands more than one gives' [Gratian's *Decretum*, c. 4, CXIV, q. 3, which borrows from the capitulary of Nijmwegen of 806], no matter what is involved, and even if one does not receive anything, if one simply hopes to receive [*Decretum*, c. 12, Comp. I, v. 15, borrowed by the decretal *Consuluit*]."[12]

One very important point must be kept in mind: usury is more than a crime, it is a *sin*. William of Auxerre states as much: "Giving for usury is in itself, and according to itself, a sin."[13] First of all, it is a sin because it is a form of *avaritia*, that is, cupidity. From the outset, Thomas of Chobham places cupidity on the spiritual level: "There are two destestable sorts of *avaritia* punishable by a judicial verdict: usury and simony [traffic in church possessions], of which I will speak next. Usury holds the first place."[14] The Dominican Stephen of Bourbon said the same thing a half-century later: "Having spoken of *avaritia* in general, I must now discuss certain of its forms, and first of all usury...."[15]

Usury is first and foremost a *theft*. In his *Homilies and Exhortations*,[16] St. Anselm (1033-1109) was the first to view the two as similar. His position was repeated in the twelfth century by Hugh of Saint-Victor, Peter Comestor, and Peter Lombard; and the equation of usury with sin finally replaced the traditional notion that usury was "shameful profit" *(turpe lucrum)*.

Usurious theft is a sin against *justice*. Thomas Aquinas states this clearly: "Is it a sin to make a charge for lending money, which is what usury is?" The reply: "Making a charge for lending money is *unjust* in itself, for one party sells the other something non-existent, and this obviously sets up an *inequality* which is contrary to *justice*."[17]

Now, perhaps even more than the twelfth century, the thirteenth century was an era of justice. Justice was the virtue par excellence of kings. The portrait of the ideal king painted by the mirror-of-princes literature stressed that the monarch must be just. With justice came progress in judicial practices and institutions, that is, royal investigators and parliaments. During St. Louis's reign, a king of France for the first time held in his left hand, in place of the *rod*, the symbolic *hand of justice*, which became the new emblem of royal power. The other Christian princes as yet carried no such emblem. Joinville left to posterity the image of the saintly king rendering justice in person beneath the oak tree at Vincennes.

At the same time, this preoccupation with *justice* became a dominant idea in the economic domain, which was so steeped in religious ideology and ethics. The *just price* and the *just wage* were the fundamental themes for economic activity, and for the marketplace then beginning to take shape. Even though the "just" price was, to be accurate, merely the market price, demand for justice was present. Usury was seen as a sin against the just price, a sin *against nature*. Such an affirmation is surprising, yet this was how thirteenth-century clerics, and the laymen they influenced, perceived the situation. The term *usury* was applied solely to collecting an interest *in money, on money*.

An astonishing text, probably dating from the fifth century and falsely attributed to St. John Chrysostom, was inserted into the Code of Canon Law during the second half of the twelfth century.

Of all merchants, the most accursed is the usurer, for (in contrast to the merchant) he sells something given by God, not something acquired by men and, after usury, he takes the thing back, along with the other person's property, which the merchant does not do. An objection will be raised: is the man who rents out a field in order to collect a share of the crops, or a house in order to collect rent, not like the man who lends his money at interest? Certainly not. First, because the sole function of the money is to pay a purchase price. Second, the tenant farmer makes the earth bear fruit and the renter occupies the house; in these two cases, the owner seems to offer the use of his property in order to collect money and, in a certain way, to exchange gain for gain, although no use can be made of the money advanced. Last, the field is gradually exhausted by use, and the house is damaged by use, while money that has been lent neither diminishes nor grows old.

Money is infertile, yet the usurer wants it to produce offspring. Having read Aristotle, Thomas Aquinas observes: *"Nummus non parit nummos"* (Money does not reproduce itself). It is not, as Jean Ibanès explains so clearly,[18] that medieval theologians and canonists refused all productivity for money, for capital; but in the case of the *mutuum*, that is, a loan at interest, it is against nature for money loaned to give birth to more money. Thomas Aquinas asserts that "money... was invented chiefly for exchanges to be made, so the prime and proper use of money is its use and disbursement in the way of ordinary transactions. It follows that it is in principle wrong to make a charge for money lent, which is what usury consists in."[19] In the same vein, St. Bonaventure holds that money is intrinsically unproductive. "In itself and by itself, money does not bear fruit but the fruit comes from elsewhere."[20]

In a sort of parable entitled "The Grapevine and Usury," Thomas of Chobham observes: "Money that lies fallow does not *naturally* produce any fruit, but the vine bears fruit *naturally*."[21] Although natural fecundity was lacking, people had nevertheless thought already about making money "work" in the early Middle Ages. In 827, Partecipazio, Doge of Venice, was already discussing *soldi laboratorii*, "money that is working." Was he referring to money lent through usury or to money "invested" for a just profit? In the thirteenth century, theologians and canonists observed with stupefaction that usurious money was indeed "working." Their disgust was echoed by the authors of collections of *exempla* and by preachers.

In his *Dialogus miraculorum*, circa 1220, an exchange between a monk and a novice, Caesarius of Heisterbach puts the following words into his characters' mouths:

"NOVICE: Usury seems to me a very grievous sin, and one most difficult to cure.

"MONK: You are right. Every other sin has its periods of intermission; usury never rests from sin. Though its master be asleep, it never sleeps, but always grows and climbs."[22]

In the *Tabula exemplorum*, a thirteenth-century manuscript in the Bibliothèque nationale of Paris, we find: "Every man stops working on holidays, but the oxen of usury (*boves usurarii*) work unceasingly and thus offend God and all the saints; and, since usury is an endless sin, it should in like manner be endlessly punished."[23]

We can imagine the popularity of this theme among preachers, and how well it lends itself to oratorical effects: Sisters, brothers, do you know of a sin that never stops, that is being committed at every moment? No? Of course you do! There is one, and only one, and I will name it. It is usury. Money given out through usury never stops working, it never stops making money. Unjust, shameful, detestable money, but money nonetheless. Brothers, do you know a worker who does not stop on Sunday or on holidays, who does not stop working while he is sleeping? No? Well, usury continues working day and night, Sundays and holidays, asleep and awake! Working while asleep? Under Satan's direction, usury, that diabolical miracle, succeeds in doing just that. In this too, usury is an insult to God and to His established order. It respects neither the natural order that He has willed for the world and for our physical life, nor the order He established for the calendar. Are not usurious coins like draft oxen, who labor unceasingly? Usury — a tireless and endless sin, a chastisement without end, an unflinching henchman of Satan, can only lead to eternal slavery, to Satan, to the endless punishment of Hell!

Today we might add that, like the nonstop factory assembly line or a modern version of the chain gang, usury inevitably ends in the eternal chains of damnation.

Making coins give birth to more coins, causing money to work without pause, in defiance of the natural laws concerning money that have been fixed by God, is that not a sin *against nature*? Were theologians not saying, especially since the "naturalist" twelfth century, *"Natura, id est Deus"* (Nature, that is to say, God)?

Great poets, who were often the best theologians on this issue, clearly understood this scandalous creature called Usury. Take, first of all, Dante, during the very century when usury was triumphant:

> *E perché l'usuriere altra via tene,*
> *per sé nature e per la sua seguace*
> *dispregia, poi ch'in altro pon la spene*

31

But because the usurer takes another way, he contemns Nature in herself and in her follower, for he puts his hope elsewhere.[24]

Or in our time, take Ezra Pound who, in the shadow of Shylock the Venetian, wrote:

Usura slayeth the child in the womb
It stayeth the young man's courting
It hath brought palsey to bed, lyeth
between the young bride and her bridegroom
CONTRA NATURAM[25]

Yes, Usury could have only one outcome: Hell. As early as the middle of the fifth century, Pope Leo I, the Great, used this formula, which echoed throughout the Middle Ages: *"Fenus pecuniae, funus est animae"* (Usurious profit from money, is the death of the soul). Usury is death.

CHAPTER III

The Thief of Time

In Romanesque sculpture from the twelfth century on, the usurer is the sole individual depicted as a criminal and displayed on a pillory. This spotlight upon him assures his preeminence among the other evil figures. It places him in the treasury of bad examples, of terrifying and salutary anecdotes that sermons introduced to the collective Christian imagination. The usurer is one of the favorite heroes of the *exempla*, those blends of the miraculous and everyday life with which preachers larded their sermons: he is the man with the moneybags.

The sculptural image and the sermon, the artistic text and the literary text: these are the sources that show the usurer as medieval men and women saw him. Take, for example, the church at Orcival, a town in the old French province of Auvergne. A modern guide to the church reads: "The first capital that attracts one's attention upon entering is the *Fol dives*, as he is named in the inscription on the abacus, so that no one will remain uninformed.... This rich man, who is by no means thin, continues to clasp his beloved moneybag. But just now devils have grabbed him. There is nothing reassuring about their bestial heads... or the way in which they clasp their victim's hair, or their pitchforks."[1] This *Fol dives*, this "rich madman," is the usurer, Hell's prey. He is obese, fattened by his usury. As if using scientific nomenclature, Stephen of Bourbon calls him the *pinguis usurarius*, the "fat usurer."[2]

From the moment of the usurer's death, the moneybag can play nasty tricks on his cadaver and give his acquaintances food for thought. Jacques de Vitry observes: "I have heard tell of a usurer who was totally unwilling to be parted from his money during a painful final illness. He summoned his wife and children and made them swear to carry out his wishes. He made them promise, on their oath, to divide his money into three parts, one of which could be used by his wife for a second marriage, while the second part went to his sons and daughters. The third part was to be put into a little bag that they were to attach to the usurer's neck and bury with him. Since he was buried with an enormous amount of money, the family wanted to get it back at night. Opening the tomb, they saw demons stuffing the usurer's mouth with coins that had been turned into red-hot coals. They fled in terror."[3] Coins move from the usurer's money pouch into the mouth of his cadaver, which has been transformed into an infernal piggybank. Here the psychoanalytic image of the medieval usurer connects money earned unjustly with oral or anal sexuality, as it does elsewhere, on the façade of a house in Goslar, for example, where a usurer is shown defecating a ducat.

In the *Tabula exemplorum*, a monkey, that caricature of a man, is given the task of purging the usurer's purse, through a ritual of inversion: "A pilgrim was aboard ship, on his way to the Holy Land, when a monkey aboard ship stole his money pouch, climbed to the top of a mast and, opening the pouch, began to sort out the contents. He set certain pieces aside and put them back into the pouch, but he threw others into the sea. When the pilgrim got his pouch back, he noticed that the monkey had thrown away all the ill-acquired coins [that is, those acquired through usury] but not the others."[4]

And finally, here is Dante's portrayal of usurers in *The Inferno*:

> *Ma io m'accorsi*
> *che dal collo a ciascun pendea una tasca*
> *ch'avea certo colore et certo segno,*
> *e quindi par che 'l loro occhio si pasca.*

> ...but I perceived that from the neck of each hung a pouch, which had a certain color and a certain device, and thereon each seems to feast his eyes.[5]

Hell is peopled by Dante's damned, with their money pouches. The words *color* and *device* refer to the coats of arms of families that Dante identified as dynasties of usurers.

First, a certain ambiguity must be eliminated. Historically the image of the usurer has been closely tied to the image of the Jew. Until the twelfth century, Jews negotiated most interest-bearing loans. These loans did not involve large sums and were carried on solely within the barter economy. That is, they loaned grain, clothing, raw materials, or objects, and received a greater amount of these items than they had originally loaned. Jews were gradually forbidden to carry on the productive activities that today would qualify as "primary" or "secondary." They either engaged in certain "liberal" professions such as medicine, long disdained by Christians, who relinquished the care of their bodies to others, with the powerful and the rich choosing Jewish physicians while the rest consulted "folk" healers or else left things to nature. Another option for the Jews was to make profit from the money that Christianity insisted must remain infertile. Since they were not Christians, they felt no scruples about lending money to individuals or to institutions outside their community, for they were violating no biblical proscriptions. Christians, on the other hand, scarcely thought of applying to the Jews a censure that was essentially intended for the family, for the Christian fraternity, for clerics first, and later for laymen. Certain monasteries, for their part, offered types of credit, especially the mortgage, which was censured at the end of the twelfth century. Indeed, everything changed in the twelfth century, first of all because economic growth led to the development of credit and to an enormous increase in the amount of currency in circulation. Certain forms of credit were accepted while others, such as the consumer loan in return for interest, were increasingly censured, and, as we have seen, old condemnations were renewed and made more specific.

The condition of Jews within Christendom worsened during this period. Pogroms took place around A.D. 1000, and again during the Crusades, perpetrated chiefly by the masses, who sought either scapegoats for calamities such as wars, famines and epidemics, or expiatory victims for their religious fanaticism. The anti-Jewish attitude of the Church stiffened and, within Christian society, from the common people to the princes, anti-Semitism — before the term existed — appeared during the twelfth and especially the thirteenth centuries. The obsession with the Jew's impurity began to spread. Accusations of ritual murder began to be made (in England at Norwich, in 1144; in France at Blois, in 1171) and then multiplied, as did accusations about profaned hosts. After going down in history as Jesus's assassins, the deicide Jews became Jesus's murderers in the Host, during this period of increasing reverence for the Eucharist. André Pezard, a leading Dante scholar, points out that for this poet, who was expressing the popular thought of his day, "usury was condemned . . . as a form of bestiality."[6] A bestial breed had its bestial practice. Christians developed an equal hatred for Jews and for usury. The Fourth Lateran Council of 1215 declared: "Wishing on this matter to prevent Christians from being treated inhumanly by Jews, we have decided . . . that if, for any pretext whatsoever, Jews have extracted heavy and excessive interest from Christians, all Christian commerce with them will be forbidden until they have atoned.[7]

As sinners, Christian usurers were under the authority of ecclesiastical courts, or tribunals of the *officialis*, which generally showed a certain indulgence toward them, leaving to God the task of punishing them by damnation. In France, usurers were Italians from Lombardy or southerners from Cahors. Thus Jews and foreigners alike were subject to the harsher and more repressive lay authority. Philip Augustus, Louis VIII, and above all the saintly Louis IX, laid down very severe laws against Jewish usurers. Thus the parallel censure of Judaism and usury contributed to fueling nascent anti-Semitism and to blackening further the image of the usurer, who was now seen as more or less indistinguishable from the Jew.

The great economic growth of the twelfth century increased the number of Christian usurers. These usurers were especially hostile to the Jews, who were sometimes formidable rivals. Although Christian usurers are my main concern, we must not forget that, during the thirteenth century, their story unfolded before a backdrop of anti-Semitism. The Church presented them as being, in theory, worse than the Jews: "Because of their wealth, usurers are honored and defended today by secular lords, who say, 'They are our Jews' [that is to say, our moneylenders, whom we protect], although they are worse than the Jews. For the Jews do not lend at usury to their brothers. Our usurers have become the intimate friends or the valets not only of lay princes but also of prelates, to whom they render services and to whom they lend money, so that their sons can be elevated to ecclesiastical benefices. Their daughters marry knights or nobles, and everything is answerable to their money. And, although in our day we scorn the poor, we honor usurers."[8] These are the remarks of Jacques de Vitry, a moralizing and pessimistic preacher who tended to paint things blacker than they really were. Being a usurer during the thirteenth century was neither so honorable nor so secure a position as Vitry implies. Behind this somber picture lay a Christian society that was a far cry from the edifying tableau that certain modern hagiographers of the Middle Ages paint for us. The truth is that, at the time of Francis of Assisi and Lady Poverty, the poor were scorned, and usury, a means of social betterment, could be held in check by the threat of Hell. Gone were evocations of the Wheel of Fortune that dips only to rise again. Replacing the wheel was the image of the ladder from which a fall was irreparable. Stephen of Bourbon borrowed an *exemplum* from a preacher of his day: "There was once, in a city, a very poor and scabby child, and he was given the nickname, 'Scabby.' As he grew older, he became a butcher's delivery boy in order to earn his bread. He accumulated a small amount of money, with which he began to practice usury. His money having multiplied, he bought slightly more respectable clothes. Then he signed a contract with someone and, thanks to usury, began to climb in both name and wealth. People began to call him Martin Scabbie, for his old nickname was becoming his family name. Then, even richer, he became Mister Martin, and, once he had become one of the richest men in the city, My Lord Martin. Finally, fattened by usury and the richest man of all, he was universally known as Monsignor Martin and everyone revered him as their lord. Unless he moves back down the rungs of that ladder, making restitution, just as he climbed it with the help of usury, he will suddenly, in an instant, descend to the depths of Hell's worst horrors."[9] This Christian usurer[10] was a sinner. But what type of sinner?

Usury is theft, so the usurer is a thief. And first of all, like every thief, he too steals property. Thomas of Chobham states this clearly: "The usurer commits a theft [*furtum*], or usury [*usuram*], or pillage [*rapinam*], for he receives foreign goods [*rem alienam*] against the 'owner's' wishes [*invito domino*], that is to say, against God's wishes."[11] But the usurer is a very particular kind of thief; even if he does not disturb public order (*nec turbat rem publicam*), his theft is especially detestable in that he is stealing from God.

What indeed does he sell, if not the time that elapses between the moment he lends the money and the moment he is repaid, with interest? Time, of course, belongs solely to God. As a thief of time, the usurer steals God's patrimony. All Chobham's contemporaries made similar statements, after St. Anselm and Peter Lombard. "The usurer sells nothing to the borrower that belongs to him. He sells only time, which belongs to God. He cannot, therefore, make a profit from selling someone else's property."[12]

More explicit, but expressing a commonplace of the period, the *Tabula exemplorum* reminds readers that "usurers are thieves, for they sell time that does not belong to them and sell someone else's property, against the owner's wishes, and that is theft."[13]

Thief of "property," and then thief of time: the usurer's position worsened. "Property" was a notion that really only put in its appearance with the Roman law of the twelfth and thirteenth centuries, a notion applied almost exclusively to personal property. "Property," then, belongs to men, but time belongs to God, and to Him alone. Throughout the epoch, church bells sang His praises, for the mechanical clock would not be invented until the late thirteenth century.

Thomas of Chobham states clearly, in the discussion of usury quoted above (p. 18): "Thus the usurer sells his debtor nothing that belongs to him, but only the time that belongs to God [*sed tantum tempus quod dei est*]. Since he sells a thing belonging to someone else, he should make no profit from it."[14]

The *Tabula exemplorum* is more explicit. It evokes the sale of days and nights, recalling their anthropological and symbolic meaning. The day is light, the setting that permits man the use of his visual senses but that also expresses the luminous matter of the soul, of the world, and of God. Night is rest, the time for tranquility, for man to rest, unless he is troubled by dreams. It is also the mystical time when instability, trouble and torment are absent. Day and night are terrestrial manifestations of the two great eschatological forces, light and peace. For, alongside the infernal night, there is the terrestrial night when one can experience a presentiment of Heaven. These are the two supreme possessions sold by the usurer.

Another thirteenth-century manuscript on the shelves of the Bibliothèque nationale of Paris portrays clearly, and more completely than the *Tabula*, the figure of the usurer as sinner and as thief: "Usurers sin against nature by wanting to make money give birth to money, as a horse gives birth to a horse, or a mule to a mule. Usurers are in addition thieves [*latrones*], for they sell time that does not belong to them, and selling someone else's property, despite its owner, is theft. In addition, since they sell nothing other than the expectation of money, that is to say, time, they sell days and nights. But the day is the time of clarity, and the night is the time for repose. Consequently they sell light and repose. It is, therefore, not just for them to receive eternal light and eternal rest."[15] So ran the infernal logic about the usurer.

This theft of time was a particularly sensitive argument for traditional clerics between the twelfth and the thirteenth centuries, a moment when values and sociocultural practices were changing, when men were appropriating bits of divine prerogatives for themselves, and when the territory under divine monopolies was shrinking. God also had to concede to men certain values of His Heaven on earth, had to grant them "liberties," "exemptions."

Another professional category was similarly transformed during the same period. I am referring to the "new" intellectuals who taught students in the city, rather than in monastic schools or cathedrals, and who, in return for their services, received the *collecta*, a payment. St. Bernard, among others, flogged them verbally, calling them "vendors, merchants of words." What they sold was knowledge, which, like time, belonged solely to God. But these thieves of knowledge would soon be vindicated, chiefly because of their *labor*. As intellectual workers, the new schoolmasters were admitted both into the accepted society of their day and into the company of the Elect, which assured the eternal existence beyond the grave of those who had been meritorious here below. In addition to the oppressed of this world, the Elect could also include privileged individuals, provided they were just and obeyed God. The Church exalted the poor, but it willingly recognized those rich men who deserved their wealth because its origins were pure and its use virtuous.

The medieval usurer found himself in a strange situation. Within a history of the *longue durée* (a history of the deeply rooted and slowly changing), the usurer is the precursor of capitalism, an economic system that, despite its injustices and failings, is part of the West's trajectory of progress. But from all contemporary points of view, in his own day this was a man in disgrace.

A long Judeo-Christian tradition condemned the usurer. For two thousand years the Scriptures had cursed him. The new values of the thirteenth century likewise rejected him as an enemy of the present. The emphasis was upon work and workers. In this context the usurer was an especially scandalous idler, for the diabolic labor of money that he initiated was but the inverse of his own odious sloth. Here again Thomas of Chobham speaks out clearly: "The usurer wants to make a profit without doing any work, even while he is sleeping, which goes against the precepts of the Lord, who said, 'By the sweat of your face shall you get bread to eat' [Gen. 3:19]."[16]

The usurer was acting counter to the Creator's plan. Medieval men initially viewed labor as a penance or a chastisement for original sin. Then, without abandoning this penitential perspective, they place increasing value upon work as an instrument of redemption, of dignity, of salvation. They viewed labor as collaboration in the work of the Creator who, having labored, rested on the seventh day. Labor, that cherished burden, had to be wrenched from the outcast position and transformed, individually and collectively, into the rocky path to liberation. The usurer, however, was a deserter from this construction site of humanity's progress.

It was during the thirteenth century that thinkers turned work into the basis of wealth and salvation, both on the eschatological level and on what we might call the economic level.

"Let each person eat the bread he has earned by his effort, let dabblers and idlers be banished,"[17] exclaimed Robert of Courçon to the usurers. And, in our day, Gabriel Le Bras observes pertinently: "The major argument against usury is that labor constitutes the true source of wealth.... The only source of wealth is mental or physical labor. There is no justification for gain other than human activity."[18]

The usurer's only chance for salvation, since *all* his gain was ill-acquired, was to make *total restitution* of what he had earned. Thomas of Chobham is very clear on this point: "Since the canonical rule states that *the sin is never pardoned unless a stolen object has been returned*, it is clear that the usurer cannot be considered a sincere penitent unless he has returned everything that he has extorted through usury."[19] Caesarius of Heisterbach says the same thing in the monk's reply to the novice: "[The sin of usury] is difficult to heal, for God does not forgive the sin of theft unless the thing stolen be restored."[20]

When discussing restitution for usury, Stephen of Bourbon and the *Tabula exemplorum* employ the same *exemplum* to show how the curse upon the usurer can extend to his heirs, if they do not make the required restitution. The usurer's friends are likewise dangerously implicated. Here is the Dominican's version of the story:

> At the time of the affair, I heard Brother Raoul de Varey, prior of the Dominicans of Clermont, tell how a usurer at death's door had repented and had called for two friends, whom he asked to be his faithful and speedy executors. They were to return the property he had acquired from others, and he required an oath from them. They took the oath, which they accompanied by imprecations. One of them called down

upon himself the sacred fire, which is called the fire of Gehenna [ergotism], and said that it should burn him if he did not fulfill his promise. The other did the same, invoking leprosy. But after the usurer's death, they kept the money, did not fulfill their promises, and fell victims to their imprecations. Under the pressure of their torment, they confessed.[21]

In the *Tabula* version, there are three faithless executors:

At his death, a usurer willed all his property to three executors, whom he charged on oath to make full restitution. He had asked them what they feared most in the world. The first had replied, 'Poverty'; the second, 'Leprosy'; and the third, 'St. Anthony's fire' [ergotism]. 'All these evils,' said the usurer, 'will fall upon you, if you do not dispose of my possessions by making restitution or distributing them as I have ordered.' But, after his death, the greedy legatees appropriated all the dead man's possessions for themselves. Without delay, the executors were afflicted by everything that the dead man had called down by imprecation: poverty, leprosy, and the sacred fire.[22]

Thus the Church gave every possible safeguard to the practice of making restitution for usury. And it dramatized the conditions under which these wishes were carried out after the usurer's death, in those cases where *post mortem* restitution seemed to have been envisaged by the penitent usurer's will — a document that would become such a precious source for studying popular attitudes toward death and the afterlife during the late Middle Ages. (The will was a kind of "passport" to the hereafter.) The Church promised the faithless executor a foretaste on earth of the torments that awaited the impenitent

44

usurer in Hell and that were transferred here below to his deceitful and greedy friends.

We are very poorly informed about actual restitution of usurious money. Historians tend to view these warnings as generally going unheeded. I would not be so naïve as to believe that restitution was a widespread practice, for we shall see that making such restitution entailed numerous difficulties; yet I think that the desire to make restitution, and the restitution itself, was greater and more frequent than is customarily believed. If we looked at the real situation more closely, we would not only be better informed about this barometer of belief and of religious feeling, but we could also measure the economic and social consequences of a phenomenon about which economic historians know all too little. We know that, in our day, the financial aspects of punishment for tax fraud are not negligible.

That making restitution was painful, especially for the greedy usurer, is revealed by a curious remark made by St. Louis and recorded by Joinville:

> He said that it was an evil thing to take what belonged to another, for the restoration of what one has taken was so irksome that just to say 'restore,' the *r*'s in it rasped your throat; and they stand for the Devil's rakes; for the Devil continually drags back to himself those who work to restore the property of others. And this he does with great subtlety, for he entices great usurers and great robbers into giving to charity what they should restore to their victims.[23]

CHAPTER IV

Death and the Usurer

The early Middle Ages had disapproved of or looked down upon many trades and professions, forbidding them first to clerics and then, in many cases, to laymen, or in any event denouncing them as pathways to sin. Appearing most often on this index were innkeepers, butchers, acrobats, actors, magicians, alchemists, physicians, surgeons, soldiers, pimps, prostitutes, notaries, and wholesale merchants; and also fullers, weavers, harnessmakers, pastrycooks, shoemakers, gardeners, painters, barbers, bailiffs, constables, customs collectors, moneychangers, tailors, perfumers, tripesellers, millers, and so forth.

We can catch fleeting glimpses of some of the reasons behind this rejection.[1] Many of these trades involved the taboos of primitive societies, for example, the taboo about blood that militated against butchers, executioners, surgeons, apothecaries, physicians and, of course, soldiers. The clerics set themselves up against the warriors. There were also taboos about impurity, about the dirt that incriminated fullers, dyers, cooks, launderers and, in Thomas Aquinas's eyes, dishwashers! And there was the taboo about money that debarred not only mercenar-

47

ies, athletes and prostitutes, but also merchants and, among them, moneychangers and, of course, usurers.

Another criterion, which was more Christian and medieval, was related to the Seven Deadly Sins. Innkeepers, bathhouse-keepers, tavernkeepers, and acrobats fostered debauchery; textile workers, with their subsistence-level wages, supplied abundant candidates for prostitution. These groups were excluded in the name of lechery. Avarice ruled merchants and men of the law, while gluttony typified the cook, pride the knight, and sloth the beggar.

The usurer, the worst type of merchant, was the object of several overlapping condemnations: handling money (which was especially scandalous), avarice, and sloth. To this can be added, as we have seen, condemnations for theft, a sin of injustice, a sin against nature. The brief against the usurer was damning.

The thirteenth century and scholasticism, its theoretical system, kept in step with the transformations in business and morality and multiplied the number of excuses for carrying on the above professions, which gradually were partially or completely rehabilitated. Occupations that were unlawful per se, by nature, were distinguished from those that were only occasionally so. The usurer profited only marginally from this casuistry. Need was ruled out, since he could only carry on usury if he already possessed money; and he could lay no claim to upright intention, since this argument only applied if the lender was planning to make restitution. Thomas of Chobham states as much, expressing his personal opinion rather than a legal or moral precept: "We believe that, just as it is permitted in extreme need to live off someone else's property in order not to die, provided one intends to make restitution when able, the usurer who experiences such great need of this sort can keep enough of his usurious gain to stay alive, but with the greatest possible parsimony, so that he will be able to return everything as soon as he can and when he has firmly decided to do so."[2]

The sole argument that could, on occasion, excuse the usurer was the argument of "communal utility," which applied to non-usurious merchants and to numerous artisans, but which rarely was admissible for usurers. And the situation became touchy when the borrower was a prince or, as we would say today, the State. Let us quote Thomas Aquinas: "The civil law leaves certain sins unpunished to accommodate imperfect men who would be severely disadvantaged if all sins were strictly prohibited by suitable sanctions. Human law, therefore, allows the taking of interest, not because it deems this to be just but because to do otherwise would hinder the 'utilities' of a great many people."[3]

The very use of the money that princes borrowed from Jewish usurers posed a problem for Thomas of Chobham. "It is surprising that the Church abets princes who with impunity transfer to their own use the money they have received from Jews, since the Jews have no other possessions than those earned by usury; and thus these princes become the accomplices of usurious practices and of usurers themselves. But the Church does not punish them, because they are powerful, which is no excuse in God's sight. True, princes claim that, since they are protecting their subjects from the Jews and from others who would chase them from their land if they could, it is consequently lawful for them to accept all this money, lent in return for their possessions."[4]

Caesarius of Heisterbach was more severe with bishops who compromised themselves with usurers.

NOVICE: There are so many usurers today, because the

bishops, who are set over the churches as watchmen, give communion to them, and give them Christian burial.

MONK: If they only concealed the vices of their flocks and did not imitate them, it would be tolerable. Some bishops today make as grievous exactions from those committed to their charge, as if they were mere secular rulers. These are the evil, the very evil fig [Jer. 24:3]. It is much to be feared that such bishops are preparing for themselves thrones by the side of the usurer's chair in Hell, for usury and violent exactions are nothing else than robbery and plunder.[5]

Thus the usurer corrupts society, at its very summit, at the very summit of the Church. The usurer is a contagious leper.

With virtually no excuses available, the usurer remained, during the thirteenth century, one of the few men whose trade was condemned *secundum se*, "in itself," *de natura*, "by its very nature." He shared this unhappy fate with prostitutes and acrobats. Thomas of Chobham stresses the similarity between the condemnations of the usurer and of the prostitute: "The Church takes action against usurers as it does against other thieves, for they engage in the public trade of usury in order to live. In like manner, the Church takes action against prostitutes, who offend God by carrying on prostitution, as a trade by which they gain their livelihood."[6] Those following these three accursed professions were, in any event, refused Christian burial and the right to give alms, two privileges granted to individuals carrying on other scorned or suspect trades.

But the usurer is the worst of all, for he sins against God in every way, not only against His person, but against nature, which He created and which is a part of Him, and also against art, which is the imitation of nature. Dante consequently placed usurers in Hell with sodomites, who also sin against nature: "And therefore the smallest ring seals with its mark both Sodom and Cahors, and all who speak contemning God in their heart."[7] Even better, as André Pezard observed in his magisterial book, *Dante sous la pluie de feu*, canto XVII of *The Inferno* places usurers in the third ring of the seventh circle, a place worse than the one reserved for blasphemers and sodomites.

Here below, the usurer lived a sort of social schizophrenia, as did the powerful butcher, so scorned by medieval cities, who would become a fervent revolutionary; as did the acrobat (and later, the actor), who was adulated although excluded; and as did the courtesans and mistresses, who, in certain periods, were sought after, feared for their beauty, their wit, and their influence over wealthy and powerful lovers, and rejected by "upright women" and by the Church. Equally courted and feared for his wealth, the usurer was scorned and cursed because of it, in a society where the worship of God excluded the public worship of Mammon.

The usurer therefore had to hide his wealth and his power. He ruled silently from the shadows. The *Tabula exemplorum* tells how it was customary, in an ancient city, for all usurers to make amends whenever the emperor visited. And so, when the latter came, all the usurers hid as best they could. But, adds the *Tabula*, "What will they do when it is God who has come to judge them?"[8]

Who, more than the usurer, fears God's scrutiny? But the usurer also fears the scrutiny of other men. In one of his *exempla*, Jacques de Vitry describes an astonishing scene: "A preacher who wanted to demonstrate to everyone that the usurer's trade was so shameful that none of them would admit to being one, said in his sermon, 'I will give you absolution according to your professional activities and your trades. All blacksmiths stand up!' And they stood. Having given them absolution, he said, 'All furriers stand,' and they stood, and so on, as he named one group of artisans after another. Finally he exclaimed, 'All usurers stand to receive absolution.' The usurers were more numerous than the people carrying on all the other trades but they hid, ashamed. To laughter and raillery, they withdrew, greatly embarrassed."[9]

But the usurer could not escape his hellish fate, even though he believed that, by giving gifts, he could buy the Church's prayers for him after his death. Here is another tale by Jacques de Vitry, who recounts how an insane usurer came back after his death in the form of one of those diabolical ghosts who abounded during the Middle Ages. The ghost took revenge upon the monks who had not kept him from going to Hell: "I have heard tell that a usurer from whom some monks had accepted a great deal of money in return for burial in their church, came out of his tomb one night, while the monks were saying matins, and grabbed a candelabrum and threw himself upon them like a madman. Amazed and terrified, the monks fled; but the ghost hit some of them on the head and broke the arms and legs of others, and, with a sort of howl, he cried out, 'Here are God's enemies and the traitors who took my money and promised me salvation, but who deceived me, for I found eternal death.' "[10]

This medieval world was fascinated by animals and, as it went about its daily affairs surrounded by symbolic fauna, it continually sought correspondences between men and animals. The usurer called a number of animals to mind. The *Tabula exemplorum*, which likens him to an ox, that heavy laborer who never stops, also compares him to a rapacious lion: "Usurers are like a lion, who rises in the morning and who never stops until he has caught his prey and has brought it back to his young. They also rob and lend money at interest in order to acquire possessions for their children."[11]

An entire bestiary of usurers can be found in Jacques de Vitry. Take the funeral of a usurer-spider: "I have heard tell that a knight once met a group of monks who were proceeding to the cemetery with a usurer's cadaver. The knight said to them, 'I will give you my spider's cadaver, and let the Devil take his soul. But *I* will get the spider's web, that is to say, all his money.' It is fitting to compare usurers to spiders, who eviscerate themselves in order to capture flies and who sacrifice not only themselves to the demons, but their sons as well, dragging them into the fires of cupidity.... This process is perpetuated in their heirs. Indeed, certain usurers assign money to their sons, even before they are born, so that it can multiply by usury; and thus their sons are born hairy, like Esau, and very wealthy. Upon their death, they leave their money to their sons, and the latter begin to wage a new war against God."[12]

Now let us turn to the fox, accompanied by the monkey: "Although the usurer has abundant wealth during his lifetime, he so lacks the viscera of charity that he does not want to make even the smallest gift to the poor, even though there is surplus wealth. He is like the fox with a big tail, a tail that is really too big and that drags on the ground. The monkey, which has no tail, asked him for a little piece of it, so that he could hide his shame. The monkey said to the fox, 'It won't hurt you to help me, for your tail is very long and very heavy.' The fox replied, 'I don't think that my tail is either long or heavy, and even if it were heavy, I would prefer to carry its weight about than to lend it to you to hide your foul rump.' These are the words of those who say to the poor, 'Why should I give you wandering beggars my money? I don't want you to eat, and I don't want to give you anything.' "[13]

And finally, there is the wolf: "It is said that the fox persuaded a thin wolf to come with him and steal, and he took him to a larder where the wolf ate so much that he could not go out the narrow hole through which he had entered. He had to fast for so long that he became as thin as before and, the worse for wear, he came out without his furry coat. Thus does the usurer leave behind, at his death, the fur coat of wealth."[14]

Was usury condemned because it was part of the censure aimed at the merchant? And was the usurer himself synonymous with the merchant? Yes and no.

It is certain that every merchant was not a usurer, and that many usurers were nothing more than usurers. Another of Jacques de Vitry's *exempla* proves this.

> I have heard tell of a usurer whom his masters wished to honor, at his death, by a farce. His neighbors tried to lift up his cadaver to bury it, but they did not succeed. One after another they tried and failed. As they all stood there astonished, a very wise old man said to them, 'So you don't know that there is a custom in this town? When a man dies, those who carry on the same trade as he, take him to the place of burial. Priests and clerics bear dead priests and clerics to the cemetery, merchants carry the merchant, butchers carry the butcher, and so forth. Let us call upon men of the same status or the same trade as this man.' They called for four usurers, who immediately lifted the body with ease and bore it to the place of burial. For the demons would not permit their slave to be carried by others than his companions in

bondage. This clearly shows the mercy of God, who 'redeems the souls of those who sin through usury and iniquity, so that having changed their name, their name becomes honorable in His sight.' We know, indeed, that no name is as detestable and as ignominious as the name usurer [*usurarius seu fenerator*]. And so they do not dare to admit their profession publicly and do not wish to be called usurers, but lenders [*commodatores*] or merchants [*mercatores*]. They say, 'I am a man who lives off his money.'[15]

It is clear that not only were the usurer and the merchant not the same man, but that one term was shameful and the other honorable, and that the term *merchant* served as a screen for the usurer. Despite everything, this proves a certain proximity, if not kinship, between the two. Indeed, I do not believe that one can say, as Raymond de Roover does,[16] that the distinction between merchant-bankers and usurers was absolute. Nor can one even assert, as John T. Noonan does, that "a banker's social standing in thirteenth-century Florence was probably at least as good as in twentieth-century New York."[17] This was perhaps true in the fourteenth and fifteenth centuries, but there were no real "bankers" in the thirteenth century, and there was no clear boundary between the activities of the merchant-banker and those of the usurer. Even in an economy and in a society where usury had dwindled, as it had in Balzac's nineteenth-century France, there certainly were differences, but not a chasm, between Gobsek, a real usurer, and old Grandet, who, along with his other business activities, carried on usury.

Besides, the usurer was the most detested type of merchant. In two of Jacques de Vitry's model sermons (numbers 58 and 59), which concern "merchants and moneychangers" (*mercatores et campores*), almost all the topics and *exempla* deal with usurers. They were undoubtedly the people most in need of salutary preaching, but this preaching was addressed to them under the label "merchants." They did not form a specific "estate" (*status*). The usurers found in Dante's *Inferno* were well-known merchants and in some cases leading merchant-bankers. The poet gives the names of several of these usurers, for example, the noble families of Gianfigliazzi and Ubbriachi, recognizable by the "devices," or coats of arms, on their pouches; the famous Scrovegni of Padua; Vitaliano del Dente, *podesta* in 1307; or Giovanni Buiamonte, "a usurer reputed to be the most terrible in Europe," but nonetheless *gonfaloniere di giustizia* in 1293. An odor of usury perpetually hovered around the thirteenth-century merchant, who had a great deal of trouble gaining recognition, not so much by the social élite as by the honorable trades.

In his model sermon *"Ad status"* 59, Jacques de Vitry provides a variant of the trifunctional society defined by Georges Dumézil and presented so clearly by Georges Duby. This interesting sermon has not, to my mind, received the attention it deserves.

> God created three types of men: peasants and other laborers to assure the subsistence of the others, knights to defend them, and clerics to govern them. But the Devil created a fourth group, the usurers. They do not participate in men's labors, and they will not be punished with men, but with the demons. For the amount of money they receive from usury corresponds to the amount of wood sent to Hell to burn them. The thirst of cupidity impels them to drink filthy water and to acquire filthy money by deceit and usury. Of their thirst Jeremiah [2:25] has said, 'Stop parching your throat.' And since, in violation of the legal interdict, usu-

rers feed upon cadavers and carcasses when they eat food acquired by usury, this food cannot be sanctified by the sign of the cross or by some other blessing; and so, as Proverbs [4:17] tells us, 'They eat the bread of wickedness and drink the wine of violence.' We read that a nun has eaten the Devil seated on a lettuce because she did not make the sign of the cross; but even worse are usurers, who, with the bread of impiety, seem to eat the Devil, whom we believe is sitting on a bite of this bread....[18]

This looseness in categories was created in order to make the trifunctional scheme correspond to the mental images of the new society. It is of some interest that the new fourth function involved the usurer, in the pejorative form of the merchant. (At a later date, others would describe this fourth category as being composed, for example, of lawyers.) Indeed, if this subdivision of the third – and economic – function by the Devil provides evidence that commercial progress was being integrated into structures of thought, it also clearly shows the intellectuals' distrust of the economic sphere. Beside the peasants and the other workers, who were vindicated because they were useful and productive, we find the Devil's function, the function of money, of harmful and unproductive usury. Before becoming the Devil's eternal prey, the usurer was his earthly friend, his protégé here below.

"It so happened that once upon a time a usurer's field remained intact, although all the land around was damaged by a storm, and, extremely happy, the usurer went to tell a priest that everything was going well for him, and to justify his way of life. The priest replied, 'That is not the way it is. Since you have acquired a great many friends in demon society, you escaped the storm they sent.'"[19] But when death approached, the friendship ended. The only thing that counted was Satan's greed for the usurer's soul. He made sure that it would not escape him. To that end, he eliminated any chance that the usurer would confess and show contrition. His first stratagem was to make the dying usurer aphasic, mute. Jacques de Vitry asserts that "when death approaches, many usurers are unable to speak and cannot confess."[20]

There was an even more radical solution: sudden death, the worst possible death for a medieval Christian, for it generally caught him in a state of mortal sin. This situation was inevitable for the usurer, who lived in a perpetual state of mortal sin. In the days of Stephen of Bourbon, the mid-thirteenth century, an astonishing news item attests to this. I am referring to the dramatic and exemplary story of the usurer of Dijon.

> It happened that, in Dijon, toward the year of Our Lord 1240, a usurer wanted to celebrate his wedding with great pomp. Led by musicians, he proceeded to the parish church of the Blessed Virgin. He stood beneath the church porch so that his fiancée could state her consent, and so that the marriage would be ratified, as was customary, by the 'words of present' [verba de presenti], before the marriage was crowned by the celebration of the Mass and by other rituals inside the church. When the bride and groom, full of joy, were about to enter the church, a statue over the porch, the statue of a usurer being carried off to Hell by the Devil, fell, with his money pouch, upon the head of the living usurer, who was about to be wed, and struck and killed him. The wedding was changed into mourning, joy was changed into sorrow. The stone usurer excluded the living usurer from the church, and from the sacraments, although the local priests,

instead of excluding him from the church, were on the contrary willing to admit him. The other usurers of the city gave money to tear down the other sculptures outside and at the back of the porch, so that another accident of this sort could not happen to them. I have seen these destroyed statues.[21]

We should really comment at length upon this text, upon the information it provides about the wedding ritual, the most important part of which still took place outside the church; upon the exclusion versus the admission of usurers; upon the connections between usurers and the clergy; upon the real and imaginary relationships between the world of the living and the world of stone church statues; and upon the group solidarity shown by urban usurers. Let us, however, restrict ourselves to the striking image of the symbolic brutality of this news item, which occurred in an actual place and on a specific date. The usurer of Dijon met his own version of the Commendatore's statue.

The guilty indulgence of certain clerics in regard to usurers did not, however, change the situation for the impenitent usurer. "At Besançon I saw," recounts Stephen of Bourbon,

> a great usurer suddenly stricken dead at the table, in the midst of a joyous feast. Seeing this, his sons by his two marriages pulled out their swords, and, completely forgetting their father, fought over his chests [full of money], which they wanted to keep and to lay hold of, caring little for their father's soul or body. He was buried in a tomb adjacent to the parish church of St. John's Cathedral. A fine tomb was constructed and inserted into the side wall of the church. In the morning it was discovered pushed far away from the church, as if to show, in this way, that he had not been in communion with the Church.[22]

Perhaps the worst way for the dying usurer to be kept away from the confessional was for him to become completely mad. Insanity led the usurer to his final impenitence. Take the story of the usurer of Notre Dame of Paris, as told by Stephen of Bourbon.

> Here is what I saw with my own eyes. When I was a young student in Paris, I went to the church of the Holy Virgin one Saturday to attend vespers. I saw a man being carried on a stretcher, suffering from a limb burned with the evil that is called the 'sacred evil,' or the 'infernal evil' [ergotism]. He was surrounded by a crowd. People close to him acknowledged that he was a usurer. And so the priests and clerics exhorted him to give up that trade and to promise that he would return his usurious gains, so that the Holy Virgin would deliver him of his illness. But he did not want to listen to them, paying no attention either to criticisms or to flattery. At the end of vespers, he persisted in his obstinacy, although this fire had spread all over his body, which had become black and swollen up, and although his eyes were bulging. He was thrown out of the church like a dog, and he died on the spot, that very evening, of that fire, still stubbornly obstinate.[23]

At the end of the Middle Ages, the *ars moriendi* engravings depict the usurer's death. But as early as the twelfth and thirteenth centuries, the *exempla* of the clerics portrayed all the struggles, all the nightmares, all the horror attendant at the dying usurer's bedside. Repentant or not, the usurer who had reached this final stage of his life was caught up in what would soon become the *danse macabre*.

Take Gottschalk, a peasant usurer from the diocese of Utrecht, of whom Caesarius of Heisterbach had heard tell. The

Crusade was being preached in his region, and he gave only five
marks when he could have donated forty without disinheriting
his children. Seated in the tavern, he scoffed at the crusaders:
"You are going to cross the sea, and waste your substance, and
expose your lives to all kinds of dangers, while I, for the five
marks with which I redeemed my vow, shall stay home with
my wife and children, and get as good a reward as you." One
night, he heard a sound like that of a grindstone in a mill adja-
cent to his house. He sent a young servant to see what was hap-
pening. The servant returned terrified and said that he had been
frozen in his tracks by terror, at the threshold of the mill. The
usurer then rose, opened the mill door, and saw a terrible vision:
there were two coal-black horses and, beside them, a horrible
man who was black, like them. He said to the peasant: "Quick!
Mount this horse; it has been brought for you." Incapable of
resisting, the usurer obeyed. With the Devil astride the other
horse, he sped through the regions of Hell. There he met his
father and his mother, and many acquaintances whom he
did not know would be in these regions. He was particularly
struck by the sight of a burgrave, whom people had thought to
be an honest knight, sitting on an enraged heifer, his back
exposed to the horns, which tore his flesh with each uncon-
trolled bounce. This fine knight had stolen his cow from a
widow. At last the peasant saw a fiery seat in which there
could be no rest, but only endless punishment for he who sat
in it. The Devil said to him, "After three days you will put
off your body, and your soul will return to your own place,
and seated in that chair you will receive your reward." His
family found the usurer in the mill, unconscious, and carried
him to his bed. Sure that he would undergo the fate he had
witnessed, he refused confession and contrition. Without con-

fession, without the viaticum, without extreme unction, he was buried in Hell.[24]

Stephen of Bourbon describes other horrible deaths meted out to usurers. Here is one that he got from Nicolas of Flavigny, archbishop of Besançon, who used to recount the tale in his sermons.

A rich usurer who was not worried about God's judgment, and who was asleep one night beside his wife after a hearty meal, suddenly rose, trembling. 'What is the matter with you?' asked his wife. 'I have just been present at the Last Judgment, and I heard countless complaints and accusations being made about me. Stupefied, I was unable to speak and to request penance. Finally, the Supreme Judge sentenced me to be handed over to the demons, who are supposed to come today to fetch me and carry me off.' He put on a jacket that was hanging on the hook, an item of little value that had been hocked by a debtor, and went out, disregarding his wife. His family followed him and found him nearly insane in a monastery church. The monks, who were chanting matins, kept him until the noon-hour service but could not get him to confess his sins, or promise restitution, or show any sign of penitence. After the mass he went out of the church and headed for home. They were walking along a river and saw a ship appear, moving upriver with great speed, but apparently with no one on board. But the usurer said that the ship was loaded with demons who were coming to carry him off and take him away. As he uttered these words, they grabbed him and put him into the ship, which immediately turned around and disappeared with its prey.[25]

The peasant usurer's phantom vessel calls to mind the ship of the Flying Dutchman.

How many usurers belonged to Hellequin's band, that death squadron whose ghostly hunters pass through the air on certain nights, their shapes distorted by the moonlight, to trouble sleep with the funereal sounds of their unearthly hunting horns, making the shadows tremble as they sob about their sins and about their anguish at endlessly wandering?

Let us immerse ourselves even deeper in horror and listen once again to Stephen of Bourbon.

> I have heard tell of a gravely ill usurer who did not want to make restitution but who nonetheless ordered that the contents of his storehouse of grain be distributed to the poor. When his servants wanted to collect the wheat, they found that it had changed into snakes. Upon learning this, the contrite usurer made full restitution and ordered that his cadaver be thrown naked into the midst of these snakes so that it would be devoured by the snakes here below, and thus avoid having his soul devoured by those in the beyond. This was done. The snakes devoured his body and left nothing but whitened bones on the spot. Some people add that, once they had done their work, the snakes disappeared and that nothing remained but bare, whitened bones, shining in the light.[26]

Here we have the usurer's surrealist skeleton. More realistic is Jacques de Vitry's account of another usurer's death, which involves a touch of black humor.

> A good priest who refused to bury a parishioner who had been a usurer and who had not made restitution before his death, serves as an inspired example. Indeed, this sort of

plague upon mankind should not receive Christian burial, and usurers are worthy of no tomb other than the sort given to donkeys.... But since the dead usurer's friends were very insistent, the priest yielded to their pressure and said, 'Let us put his body on a donkey and see God's will, and what He will do with the body. Wherever the donkey takes it, be it a church, a cemetery or elsewhere, there will I bury it.' The body was placed upon the donkey which, without deviating either to right or left, took it straight out of town to the place where thieves are hanged from the gibbet, and with a hearty buck, the donkey sent the cadaver flying into the dung beneath the gallows. The priest left it there, with the thieves.[27]

In our day Luis Buñuel has portrayed the cadavers of the poor *olvidados*, abandoned on public garbage heaps, but, unlike them, the usurer deserved being thus forgotten.

Even though it changes over the ages, the quintessential model of the usurer is the one described by Eudes of Sully, bishop of Paris between 1196 and 1208: "There was in France a usurer whose manservant was called Hell and whose womanservant was called Death. He died suddenly and had, as gravediggers, only Hell and Death."[28]

CHAPTER V

Your Money and Your Eternal Life:

Purgatory

The Church and lay power would say to the usurer, "Choose! Your money *or* your life." But the usurer would think, "What I want is my money *and* my life." Impenitent usurers who, at the moment of their deaths, preferred to keep ill-acquired money or even to carry it off with them to the grave, scoffing at the hell that had been forecast for them, must have been in the minority. One might even ask whether they were not imaginary usurers, an invention of ecclesiastical propaganda intended to make the message more telling. Only nonbelief could explain an attitude of this sort, and the thirteenth-century nonbeliever appears to have been a hypothetical rather than a real person. The impenitent usurer was undoubtedly either an improvident usurer who, despite the Church's warnings, was surprised by death, or else he was an optimistic usurer, who was counting on the forgiveness of a God who was more understanding than the Church.

The thirteenth century was a period in which values became increasingly worldly. Before then men and women had, of course, given themselves over to the things of this world and been enticed into sin by the charm of earthly pleasures; they lived in a society that had never been completely Christianized, where religion had perhaps imposed its law on the surface of beings and things but had not fully changed consciences and hearts. Christianity was, in short, tolerant. It expected clerics, and particularly monks — an élite of "saints" who alone were suited to a perfect respect for religion and its values — to do penance for all the others and to tolerate their superficial Christianity on condition that they show respect for the Church, for its members, and for its possessions, and on condition that periodic public penance be carried out, and on occasion, spectacular penance for shocking sins. It was a Christianity that, despite its internal quest for God, asked little more of laymen than that they control their brute nature. For laymen were violent and unlettered; they were warriors full of *superbia*, that is, pride, who participated in massacres, plunder and rape; or they were workers, especially peasants, who differed little from the animals tormented by *envy*, and who had been designated by God to serve the two chief orders of society, as Ham had been forced to serve Japheth and Seth.

The lay world was one of savage violence. In the face of this violence, the Church, with the help of kings and emperors, tried to impose order, external order. A code or preestablished penance was applied to sins, a code inspired by the punishments decreed by barbarian law. A person did not improve his character, rather he redeemed his errors. The monastic ideal was *contemptus mundi*, scorn for the world, refusal to live in the world. But this was a matter for monks. For laymen, God was far distant, and the surrounding world, harsh and beset by famines, illness and war, was on the whole not very appealing. Only the powerful had reasons to enjoy life, and they thanked God, guarantor of their power, for a few favors. The Church

66

told the powerful and the weak that the world was growing old, was settling into a state of ruin, and that they must think of their salvation. The majority of laymen believed that the mighty had taken full advantage of the little time that remained, while the humble must pry from this earth the crumbs of pleasure within their reach. There was, of course, God and the Last Judgment. But men did not manage to discern a close link between their life and God's eventual judgment of each one of them. This God resembled the ravenous gods whom their ancestors had long adored, gods who were either natural forces such as oak trees, springs, or rocks that had either been destroyed or been baptized by the Church, or else idols that priests and monks had overturned and replaced by churches and statues. He was an entirely different God, but one whom the mass of superficially Christianized laymen sought to satisfy by the same offerings or by new gifts that resembled the old ones. The powerful and the rich gave land, money, golden objects or rents; the poor gave humbler gifts, among them some of their children, the oblates of the monasteries. Since this was a subjugated population, the peasants, who were in the majority, were made to pay the greater part of a burdensome offering, the tithe, a tenth of their harvest. God was represented on earth by His saints and by the Church. It was to them that laymen offered these "gifts."

A great change took place around A.D. 1000, which we designate as the feudal system (*féodalité*). It undoubtedly increased injustices and inequalities, but it gave the masses a certain security, from which a relative well-being was born. The Church reconsidered its relation to this new society. On the one hand, it tried to extricate itself from its involvement in the world. On the other, it tried to make society truly Christian. To do so, it used the carrot and the stick, the customary method of the powerful.

The stick was Satan. A native of the distant and mysterious East, the Devil was rationalized and institutionalized by the Church and began to play his role effectively about 1000. As God's scourge, general of a well-organized army of demons, and master of his kingdom of Hell, the Devil was the orchestra conductor of feudal imagery. But, since God in Heaven of necessity admitted only a minority of the perfect and saintly, the Devil could merely offer an afterlife devoid of hope to a society that was increasingly unable to think in terms of the strictly antagonistic model of good people and bad people, or black and white.

The unpitying and Manichean society of the early Middle Ages was becoming unlivable. The masses imposed the movement for *peace* upon the Church, which imposed it upon the aristocracy and the princes, who sought to turn it to their own advantage. This movement for peace would, for example, be transformed into the "duke's peace" in Normandy, and into the "king's peace" in France. No, this earth had to be more than a vale of tears, an expectation of the Apocalypse! As early as 1000, Raoul Glaber, a Cluniac monk, expressed his astonishment at a new white mantle of churches. This mantle was not the snows of winter, but the blossoms of spring. Improved and cultivated, the earth became more productive. Machines such as looms, mills, and plows with wheels and mold-boards appeared, as did tools such as the harrow and the iron plowshare. Technology brought improved plowing and cultivation of vineyards, led to cams that transformed a continuous motion into an alternating one, or ushered in the symbolic numbers of arithmetic and, at its side, a real mania about counting that, according to Alexander Murray, developed around 1200. None of this was considered *progress*. (That term would not be used until the eighteenth century.) It was perceived as growth. History, which was at a near standstill, started up again; and life on earth could be, indeed was supposed to be, the beginning, the apprenticeship for an ascent toward God. Humanity could be saved if it collaborated in God's creative work here below, for why else would God have created the world, and men and women? The carrot was *Purgatory*. Purgatory was born at the end of the Gregorian reform, that great transformation willed by the Church in order to modify all of society.

The first phase of this mutation was painful for the usurer. Although not committing a sin according to either the Jewish law or the Christian one, the Jewish usurer, increasingly driven to usury by Christian society, was experiencing a period of increasing anti-Semitism, based upon latent anti-Jewishness fanned by the struggle against usury undertaken by the Church and by the Christian princes. The Christian usurer had chosen money, the most detested of all the earthly values that were gaining ascendancy — detested even though, materially, it was becoming increasingly sought after. I am not presenting the Christian usurer as a victim, but as a guilty man who shared his offense with the whole of society, which scorned him and persecuted him while at the same time using him and sharing his greed for money. I do not prefer hypocrisy over greed. In both cases, a certain lack of awareness is no excuse. In *Das Kapital*, Marx pointed out the degree to which usury subsists in capitalism.

In this book, I am trying to show how an ideological obstacle can fetter or delay the development of a new economic system. I believe that this phenomenon can better be understood by examining closely the men who were the actors, rather than by looking solely at economic systems and doctrines. I am challenging an older history of the economy, and of economic thought, that has outlived its usefulness. I see this history as especially ineffective for the Middle Ages, because at that time the Church had no economic doctrine, and there were no economic thinkers. However, in their discussions of religious questions, including the *sin* of usury, the Church, the theologians, the canonists, and (let us not forget them) the preachers and confessors of the Middle Ages, reveal religion's impact upon phenomena that we today would call "economic." By failing to recognize the specific character of medieval behavior and thought, economic theories and histories of modern economic thought have closed their eyes to a genuine understanding of the past (there are some fortunate exceptions) and have therefore also deprived us of any light that the past can shed on the present. As great a poet as Ezra Pound perhaps did not struggle sufficiently against an outdated imagination when evoking a usurious nineteenth century, but no one expressed better than he what usury and the usurer were historically.

The historian, who must avoid eclecticism, has, however, few opportunities to propose a satisfying explanation if he looks for a single dominant cause. Many a sad offspring of Marxism has died of this reductive and aberrant belief. Clearly the usurer's salvation was due to other things than Purgatory. But before emphasizing this element, which I consider to have been decisive but complementary, we must explore the other paths that led to acceptance of the usurer. There are two paths: a *moderating* of the practice of usury, and the appearance of *new values* in the realm of economic activities.

Texts of the period expressed a blanket condemnation of usury. We know that principles are rarely carried over integrally into reality. Usury and interest are two different things, and the

Church never censured every form of interest. During the thirteenth century, a century obsessed with keeping accounts, the amount of interest charged for a loan determined to a large extent the attitudes of the authorities and of society toward usurers.

Even with rules established by the Church, which took the *market* price as the basis for the *just* price, the interest rate depended in part upon the law of supply and demand and was a partial barometer of economic activity. "In general," writes Gérard Nahon, "the further a country advances along the path toward economic development, the lower the interest rate. In Austria, a privilege granted in 1214 fixed the rate at 8 deniers a week, that is, at 74 percent, an indication of the underdevelopment of that country."[1]

Indeed, usury does not seem to have been routinely censured when it stayed within the interest rate observed for contracts in which interest was tolerated. The market rate was accepted, within certain limits, through a sort of regulating that used the market as its point of reference, but that also imposed brakes upon it. How could the Church refrain from interfering? Even if it frequently acquiesced to people in power, it still wanted as much control as possible and sought the real exercise of one of its essential functions, that is, the protection of the poor, with whom it identified in its ideals, although in practice this identification was not very strict.

The Church was also the memory of the past. Roman law, alternating with the Byzantine-Christian legislation of Justinian and with the barbarian laws of the early Middle Ages, authorized a usury of 12 percent a year; and the rate of $33\frac{1}{2}$ percent must have become the authorized ceiling between the year 1000 and the thirteenth century, for this is the rate that two French kings, Louis XVII (1223) and St. Louis (1230 and 1234), imposed upon Jewish usurers. The interest rates observed during the thirteenth century in the great Italian marketplaces were often even lower than that. In Venice, they habitually ranged from 5 to 8 percent. But there were places, such as Austria, where it was high. Although rates generally remained between 20 and 30 percent in Florence, they could go up to 40 percent at Pistoia and at Lucca. Philip the Fair's inquiry of 1284 reveals that *Lombard* moneylenders, who were often likened to Jews and to people from Cahors, that is to say, to usurers, asked interest rates that ranged from 34 percent to 266 percent. On the other hand, R.H. Helmholz's excellent study of usury in thirteenth-century England demonstrates that, although rates varied from 5½ percent to 50 percent, the interest in the majority of loans ranged from 12 percent to 33⅓ percent.

In fact, even official texts explicitly condemn only those usurers who were excessive. In 1179, the Third Lateran Council singled out only those usurers who were "manifest" *(manifesti)*, who were "common" *(communes)* or "public" *(publici)*. I believe that it was a question here of usurers whose *fama*, whose "renown" or public reputation, considered them not as amateur usurers, but as "professionals," and above all as carrying on *excessive* usury.

Once again condemning Jewish usurers, the Fourth Lateran Council of 1215 referred only to those who were "heavy and excessive" *(graves et immoderatas)*.

In general, the condemnation of usury was linked to the condemnation of excess by Canon Law, for example in sales contracts under the category of *laesio enormis*, "enormous damages," a term borrowed from Roman law.

This notion of *moderation* is merely a specific example of the ideal of *measure* that, from the twelfth to the thirteenth century, imposed itself upon morals and theology, from Hugh of Saint-Victor to Thomas Aquinas, within the context of historical evolution and of the "twelfth-century renaissance," which once again valorized ancient authors. In the mid-thirteenth century, the saintly Louis IX both observed and praised the *juste milieu* in everything, in clothing, in food, in worship, in war. For him, the ideal man was the *prudhomme*, the man of integrity, who could be distinguished from the brave knight because he linked wisdom and *measure* to prowess. The moderate usurer therefore had some chance of slipping through the meshes of Satan's net. His other chance lay in the fact that the forbidden and outlawed part of his territory was shrinking. New practices and new values, which were developing in the field that we today call the economy, restricted usury's domain. Scholastic tradition therefore determined that there were five *excuses*.

The first two were related to the notion of *indemnity*. One was the *damnum emergens*, the unexpected appearance of a penalty caused by a delayed repayment. This justified the collection of interest that was no longer usury. The other excuse was the *lucrum cessans*, that is to say, greater legitimate profit could have been earned by the usurer had he invested more advantageously the money he lent at usury.

The third excuse, and, in the eyes of the Church, the most important and legitimate one, held that usury could be considered a salary, a remuneration for *labor (stipendium laboris)*. This vindicated university teachers and non-usurious merchants. Teaching a science is tiring, and it supposes an apprenticeship and methods that depend upon labor. Journeying by land and sea, going to fairs, and even keeping books or changing money, is also labor and deserves a salary.

In a less obvious, and above all in a less usual way, the usurer

can also labor. He labors not so much while lending and collecting the money that was producing new wealth, against nature,
constantly, even at night, without causing fatigue, as while
acquiring the money that he lends at usury and while putting
the usurious money to use — not by giving it away, which is a
praiseworthy but slothful practice, but by carrying on a truly
productive activity.

The two final excuses were associated with *risk*, a relatively
new value of Christian society. Of course, this value existed
earlier, in the risk taken by a monk such as St. Anthony, who
exposed himself in solitude to particularly dangerous assaults
by Satan; in the risk taken by a warrior such as Roland, who
faced death in order to defend the Church and the faith and,
within a feudal society, his lord; and in the risk taken by a layman who was ready to sacrifice his life and his possessions along
the land and sea routes taken by a pilgrim or, above all, by a
crusader. This new risk was economic and financial and took
the form of the danger of losing the *capital* one had lent *(periculum
sortis)*, of not being reimbursed, owing either to the debtor's
insolvency or to his bad faith. The second excuse involving risk
is the more interesting and, like the first risk, was contested by
certain theologians and canonists. It involves the degree of uncer-
tainty *(ratio incertitudinis)*. Influenced by the Aristotelianism then
permeating theology and Canon Law after 1260, this notion
recognized the *certain* and the *uncertain* in planning and in economic calculations, and it was to play a great role in the subsequent establishment of capitalism.

So an increasing number of usurers had some chance of being
saved from Hell, either through moderation or through having
shifted their activity to the new areas where lending at interest
was authorized. But many usurers were still threatened with

74

Hell by reason of their practices, notably their consumer loans. Now, they themselves had not remained untouched by the religious changes that had been going on throughout the twelfth century, and they too were worried about the new forms of confession, contrition and redemption. Did the newly drawn landscape of the hereafter at the end of the twelfth century offer them a chance of salvation?

I will evoke here only briefly what I have analyzed at length in my book *The Birth of Purgatory*. From the majority of ancient religions, Christianity had inherited a two-part afterlife. One part, Paradise, was for reward, and the other part, Hell, was for punishment. It had also inherited a God who was both good and just, who was a merciful and severe judge and who, having given man a certain degree of free choice, punished him when he chose badly and, at that point, abandoned him to Satan, the spirit of evil. Whether a man went to Paradise or Hell depended on the sins he had committed here below, a place of penance and trials for humans tainted by original sin. The Church kept a more or less close rein on this process of salvation or damnation, through exhortations and warnings, and through penance that freed men from the burden of their sins. Only two verdicts were possible: Paradise or Hell. The verdict would be uttered by God (or by Jesus) at the Last Judgment and would be effective for eternity. From the earliest centuries of the Church, Christians, as funeral inscriptions reveal, hoped that a dead man's fate was not definitively sealed at his demise, and that the prayers and the offerings — that is, the *intercession* — of the living could help dead sinners escape Hell or, at least, benefit from less harsh treatment than that meted out to the worst inmates of Hell, as they waited for the final sentence at the Last Judgment.

But there was no precise knowledge about any eventual

redemption after death, and belief in redemption remained vague, chiefly owing to confusion about the geography of the infernal regions, where no specific receptacle existed for those whose admission to Heaven or to Hell had been delayed. The authors of numerous accounts of real or visionary trips to the hereafter did identify a specific spot where the sins that had not yet been effaced and expiated were redeemed after death. Those writers so privileged were conducted by an authorized guide, in most cases the archangels Raphael or Gabriel or an important saint such as Paul, but also, subsequent to Purgatory's birth, by Virgil, who served as Dante's guide during the rebirth of classical culture. They tended to portray two hells, a lower one, and an upper one for those damned who were less guilty. Mistrustful, the Church kept close watch over these travel accounts, which had been inherited from Jewish and Christian apocalyptic traditions, often verging on the heretical, which circulated within monastic culture, despite their being permeated with a "popular" culture that smacked of the "pagan."

When, during the rise of the West, between the year 1000 and the thirteenth century, men and the Church began to find the simplistic contrast between Heaven and Hell unbearable, and when conditions were ripe for defining a third place in the hereafter where the dead could be purged of a residue of sins, a word appeared, *Purgatorium*, Purgatory, to designate this place that had at last been identified. I would remind you that Purgatory is a part of the interiorization of religious feelings that, from intention to contrition, demands an internal conversion of the sinner, rather than external acts. It is also part of a socialization of religious life that pays more attention to the members of a social and professional group than to the components of the social order. Lastly, it is part of a general tendency to avoid confrontations resulting from a reductive dualism. Between the poles of good and evil, of superior and inferior, it picks out middle positions, intermediary positions. And, among the sinners, it identifies some who are neither totally good nor totally wicked — an Augustinian distinction — and who are, for the moment, destined neither for Paradise nor for Hell. If they have sincerely repented before their death, these sinners are now burdened solely with venial sins and with the residue of mortal sins that are still regretted, if not a sentence for eternity. For a certain period they will stay in a place called Purgatory, where they will suffer punishment comparable to the torment of Hell, and these punishments will, as in Hell, be inflicted by demons.

The duration of this painful stay in Purgatory does not depend solely on the quantity of the sins still burdening them at the moment of their death, but upon the affection shown by their loved ones. Be they blood relatives or artificial relatives, such as confraternities to which the deceased had belonged, religious orders to which they had been benefactors, or saints for whom they had shown special reverence, loved ones could shorten a dead person's stay in Purgatory through prayers, offerings, and intercession. Thus solidarity between the living and the dead was heightened.

The dead in Purgatory also benefited from the supplementary section added to their biography, described so precisely by Philippe Ariès and Pierre Chaunu. Above all, they were sure that, when their purifying trials had ended, they would be saved and go to Paradise. Indeed, Purgatory *has only one door*, the door to Paradise. The important decision is made when the dead person is sent to Purgatory. He knows that he will be saved in the end, by the very latest at the Last Judgment.

The birth of Purgatory made the approach of death, or of one's final moments, highly dramatic. Immediately after death, when the *individual* judgment takes place, God utters his momentous decision: Paradise, Hell, or Purgatory. This was, therefore, an individual sentence, for a very individualized death in which the dead man was responsible for his fate. The usurer's last moments were, in this respect, particularly painful. As a member of a profession that had by nature remained unlawful, and also as an individual, he was one of the living damned who were drawing near the mouth of Hell. Would he escape at the last moment? What terrible suspense.

Purgatory was not consciously or explicitly discovered in order to depopulate Hell. But this is what tended to occur in practice. In order to combat this tendency toward laxity, the thirteenth-century Church stressed the infernal nature of the punishments of Purgatory, although it did not change the final outcome, Paradise.

Now, isn't the usurer a "totally wicked" person? Well, here is what we find in the final chapter of Caesarius of Heisterbach's *Dialogus miraculorum*, written about 1220. This Cistercian monk presents an approximately equal number of *exempla* portraying the dead in Hell, in Purgatory, and in Paradise. In one corner of Purgatory we suddenly find an unexpected, unheard-of resident, a usurer:

> MONK: A certain usurer of Liège died recently and was forbidden burial in the cemetery by the bishop. But his wife went to the Apostolic See and begged for his burial there and when the pope refused, she pleaded in this way for him: "I have heard tell, lord, that man and wife are one and that the Apostle says an unbeliever can be saved by the believing

wife. Hence whatever shortcomings there may have been in may husband, I, who am part of his flesh, will most gladly make up for these and give satisfaction to God for his sins." And the cardinals pleading her cause, by order of the lord pope, the man is restored to the cemetery. Hard by his grave she had a house made for herself, in which she shut herself up and by alms, prayer and fasting and by watching day and night strove to please God for his soul's sake. But when seven years were gone, he appeared to her in a black dress and thanked her, saying: "God reward thee, for I have been rescued from the pit of Hell and from the greatest pains by thy efforts. But if for still another seven years, thou wilt confer like benefits upon me, I shall be entirely freed." And when she had done so, again appearing to her in a white dress and with joyful face, he said: "Thanks to God and to thee that today I am delivered."

NOVICE: Why did he say he was freed from the deep of Hell, where there is no redemption in it?

MONK: The deep of Hell means the bitterness of Purgatory. It is like a prayer which the church makes for the dead: "Lord Jesus Christ, King of Glory, deliver the souls of all the faithful dead from the power of Hell and from the pit of the lake, etc." It does not pray for the damned, but for those that are to be saved; and the power of Hell or the pit of the lake or the mouth of the lion is understood as the bitterness of Purgatory. By no means would the usurer have been freed from punishment, if he had not repented at the end.[2]

And so we have the ghost of a usurer. Purgatory is also a place where ghosts are sorted out. From it issue those ghosts for whom God permits or orders a brief return to earth to prove

79

the existence of Purgatory and to beg their dear ones to hasten their deliverance by their suffrage, as did the usurer of Liège. They must be heeded. On the other hand, unauthorized ghosts must be chased away, but their wretched fate can also teach a lesson. Take the usurious knight described by Caesarius:

> A certain knight at his death bequeathed his property acquired by usury to his son. One night he knocked loudly at the door and when a page ran and asked why he knocked, he replied: 'Let me in, I am the lord of this land,' and gave his name. The boy looked through the grille and recognizing him said: 'My master is certainly dead, I will not let you in.' And when the dead man went on knocking without any effect, at last he said: 'Take these fish on which I live, to my son; look you, I am hanging them on the door.' In the morning, when they went out, they found in a sort of bundle a quantity of toads and snakes. In fact this is the food in Hell and it is cooked in the sulphurous flames.[3]

There is, to be sure, a way for the usurer to escape from Hell and even from Purgatory: he must make restitution. Stephen of Bourbon stresses this: "If the usurer wishes to avoid damnation, he must *cough up* [the term is a very strong one, *evomat*, which means to vomit it up], in restitution, the dishonestly acquired money and confess his fault. Otherwise, he will *cough them up* [by vomiting, *emovet*, doubtlessly to be interpreted literally] during his punishments in Hell."[4] Restitution and confession, in the temporal and in the spiritual. But he must make full restitution, and in time. Now, not only did many usurers hesitate and remain reticent until it was too late, but this restitution was, in addition, not always easy to carry out. Perhaps the usurer's victim had died, and his heirs could not be found. Coming up with the money that had been earned through usury could be difficult, especially if it had been spent or had been invested in a purchase that could not be cancelled or recuperated. Usury is founded upon time. The usurer had sold time, had stolen it, and this theft could only be forgiven if he returned the stolen object. Could one, in order to make restitution, turn the clock backwards? Steeped in this temporal dimension of economic practices involving currency, medieval men found it harder to go back in time than they did to go forwards.

The problem was especially difficult if the usurer left a widow and children. This issue preoccupied theologians and canonists. At this point the last and most important character comes on stage, the *usurer's wife*, his soon-to-be *widow*. Here is how Thomas of Chobham tells it:

> What does one say about the wife of a usurer who has no resources other than those earned by usury? Should she leave him because of his incorrigible spiritual fornication, or should she remain with him and live off usurious money?
>
> There are two opinions.
>
> Some say that she should live by the work of her hands, if she knows a trade, or by her friends' resources. If she has neither friends nor a trade, she can also leave her husband, as much on the grounds of spiritual fornication as of corporal fornication, for she does not owe her body's service to such a husband, she would be like an idolatress, for cupidity [*avaritia*] means *serving idols* [Eph. 5:5].
>
> Others say that she should instead do as the Lord did, who ate with sinners and thieves who gave him nothing but other people's property, but who was Himself the spokesman for the poor and who persuaded thieves to return the

things they had stolen [Luke 19] and who thus ate their property lawfully. In like manner, the usurer's wife can persuade her husband to make restitution for his usury or to take a smaller amount of usury from the poor [*vel minores usuras accipiat a pauperibus*], and by working for them and by pleading their cause, she can lawfully live off their property.[5]

Note the allusion here to toleration of moderate usury, "petty" usury.

The following text involves children:

> Take someone who owns nothing but the product of usury and who would like to repent. If he makes restitution of everything he owns, his daughters would have to become prostitutes and his sons bandits, and he himself would beg and his wife would abandon him. Can the Church not give him some advice so that he does not have to make full restitution? We say that it would be good advice to have him ask those to whom he ought to make restitution to consider the debt paid. If he does not obtain that favor, we believe that, since every man in extreme need can live off someone else's property without dying, as we have said above, provided he intends to make restitution when he can, the usurer himself, when in need, can keep enough of his usurious money to live, on condition that he lives with great parsimony and that he firmly intends to make total restitution when he can.[6]

Once again we encounter here the value of *intention* and the excuse based on *necessity*.

The wife plays a major role in all matters relating to the usurer's eternal fate. She must strive to persuade him to renounce this cursed trade and to return the money that will doom him to Hell. Many usurers' wives do this in *exempla*. The wife is usually a touching figure, worthy of attention, akin to Balzac's women who lived in the shadow of a loan-shark husband or father, sometimes so terrified that they dared not speak to them, much less criticize them, and tried instead to redeem the man's ignominy in the shadows of prayer. The Church has always portrayed the wife in two ways. Sometimes she is denounced as the Eve who made Adam succumb to temptation, and sometimes she bears within her the hope of converting or improving her evil husband.

But, within this situation, the marital roles played by husband and wife intersect, as do the images of them held by the Church and by society. Georges Duby, among others, has brilliantly demonstrated that the conception and practice of marriage were changing at that moment, as part of a general mutation. Without going into detail, we can state that the woman seems to have benefited from this transformation. The monogamous and indelible ecclesiastical model of marriage changed. It evolved into a sacrament and was based upon the couple's *mutual* consent and carnal consummation. This contract thus gave the woman increased participation and protection. Does not the wife of the usurer from Liège exemplify the "new" couple, as she proudly reminds the pope of the Church's definition of marriage, and as she cites St. Paul, "Man and woman are one flesh"? Within the general reform in which it was engaged, the Church hesitated to retain any of the old laws that could support collective responsibility. The money that a man earned from usury within the context of a social economy became the couple's money within their familial domestic economy. How can the husband be punished without punishing the wife? The *exemplum* of the usurer from

83

Dijon provides a vivid answer to this question, but this answer is not very useful in daily life. The statue falls down, kills the usurious husband and spares the wife before the marriage has been consummated.

CHAPTER VI

The Heart Has Its Own Tears

Let us then follow the wife of the usurer of Liège along the path to salvation. It is an extreme example since, having made her proud marital claims, she redeemed her usurious husband through her own personal sacrifices and received no thanks or encouragement beyond a ghost's gratitude and a rather crude incarnate vision of an *arithmetic* of the Purgatory system. The ghost's body was a black-and-white barometer of the time spent in Purgatory. In other texts, the top half of the body of the half-purged dead person is white, while the bottom half is black. Being half-black and half-white means that the midpoint has been reached.

Here is another, and more modest, "good woman" married to a usurer: "I have heard tell of a good woman who had a usurer as a husband. She asked him assiduously to make restitution and to become one of Christ's poor rather than one of the Devil's rich. He would not agree, but he was suddenly arrested by his lord here below and was only released when he gave, as ransom, the money he had acquired by usury. He was freed, but his wife wept very bitterly. He reproached her for it. 'Well! I am poor, just as you wished.' But she replied, 'I am not weeping because you are poor but because, with the disappearance of the money with which you were supposed to make restitution, your sin remains upon us, though it should have been washed away by restitution and repentance.'"[1]

It often happened, moreover, that the woman's efforts were in vain. Let us return to the story of the usurious peasant from the diocese of Utrecht. When he entered the neighboring mill, Gottschalk encountered the Devil, who took him to see the seat that was reserved for him in Hell. Yet he did not repent. Here are the details about his end, subsequent to his return from the trip to Hell: "The priest was summoned in haste, at the wife's request, and she begged him to calm his terrors, to deliver him from despair and to exhort him to the way of salvation. But when the priest urged him to contrition for his sins, and to make an honest confession, assuring him that none need despair of the mercy of God,"[2] the usurer, convinced that he was damned, refused all contrition, confession and extreme unction, and was buried in Hell. His wife did not give up. "The priest refused to give the Church's burial, but his wife bribed him, and he was laid in the cemetery. For this the priest was afterwards accused before the Synod of Utrecht, and was duly punished."[3]

Rather than surrender to sanctimonious admiration for the attitude shown by usurers' widows, I prefer to point out that there were also some "bad" wives. Jacques de Vitry tells the tale of a knight who had been stripped of his possessions by a usurer and imprisoned at his instigation. The knight married the usurer's widow and, thanks to her, enjoyed all his wealth.

Stephen of Bourbon evokes the conduct of the wife of a usurer of Besançon: "During his last moments, he did not want to write a will or to give alms, but left all his possessions at his wife's disposal. As soon as he died, the wife notified one of his enemies and married him. An honest woman reproached her for it, pointing out that her husband was not yet cold in his grave. She replied, 'If he is warm, blow upon him.' These were the only alms she would give for his soul."[4]

The traditional system of redemption available to the usurer during his life, and even at death's door, included confession, contrition (or repentance) and satisfaction (or penance). In his case, penance meant making restitution. But, from the twelfth to the thirteenth century, the conception of the sin and of the penance it entailed increasingly emphasized *contrition*. Hard-pressed by death, unable to confess because the Devil had robbed him of speech, and lacking the time to make restitution, the usurer managed to save himself by sincere contrition. In extreme cases, certitude about the sincerity of his contrition was not even necessary. God knew the truth and sometimes made it known on earth by a sign. Since contrition without penance led to Purgatory, and since Purgatory was in any event a harsh trial, why not give the usurer credit for his contrition?

Take the usurer of Liège. He did not confess; he did not make restitution. His wife paid not with his money, but with her own person, and with alms. Caesarius of Heisterbach's *exemplum* concludes by stating that the usurer therefore had "repented in the end."

The attempt to wrench this contrition from the usurer could fail. Here is the story of St. Dominic's failure and of the final deceitfulness of a falsely contrite usurer. "In the book of an elderly brother," says Stephen of Bourbon,

> I read that, in Lombardy, St. Dominic was requested by certain persons to visit a man of the law, an important lawyer and a usurer, who was gravely ill. In the presence of a priest,

the saint urged him to return his usurious gain. But the usurer refused, saying that he did not want to leave his sons and his daughters in poverty. And so St. Dominic withdrew with the others and with Christ's body. Troubled, the usurer's friends asked him to promise [to repent] until he had confessed and so that he would not be refused a Christian burial. He promised, thinking that he was fooling them. As they were going out after having given him communion, he began to scream that he was on fire and that Hell was in his mouth. 'I am burning up competely,' and lifting his hand, he said, 'This is burning up entirely,' and did likewise with his other limbs. That is how he died and was consumed.[5]

Consider, on the other hand, the contrition and penance obtained from a usurer and a murderer by a skillful confessor. During Lent, while he was hearing the confession of an old lady, a priest of St. Martin's Church of Cologne saw two of his parishioners sitting opposite him, chatting in front of a window. One was a usurer, the other a murderer. The old woman left, and the usurer came to confess.

The priest said to him, 'My friend, you and I together today will defeat the Devil finely. Only do you confess your sins without reserve, put away all intention of sinning again and follow my advice, and I promise you eternal life; and I will so moderate your penance that it shall not be too difficult for you.' For he knew well the sin by which he was beset. He replied: 'If I could really be sure of what you promise, gladly would I follow your advice.' And the confessor renewed his promise. Now when he had made his confession, forsworn his usury, and undertaken his penance, he went to his companion, the homicide already spoken of, and said: 'Truly, we have the kindest of priests, for he has brought me to repentance by the gentleness of his words.' The other, urged by his example, came to confession, and perceiving the same atmosphere of compassion around him, accepted his penance and carried it through.[6]

The story is mawkish, but it reveals a desire to save the usurer even if it meant being lenient.

Yet the very same Caesarius of Heisterbach notes that the usurer is very hard to save, and that repentance without restitution is of dubious value. "[The sin of usury] is difficult to heal, for God does not forgive the guilt of theft unless the thing stolen has been restored. The fornicator, the adulterer, the murderer, the perjurer and the blasphemer, all receive forgiveness from God, as soon as they show contrition for their sin; but the usurer, although he may be sorry for his sin, does not obtain pardon, so long as he keeps the fruit of the usury when he might restore it."[7]

Repentant and doubting, the dying or newly dead usurer was sometimes the object of a ferocious battle between devils and angels. An old Benedictine monk of Saxon origins told Caesarius of Heisterbach the tale of a very wealthy usurer who held the art treasures of various churches as collateral. Smitten by a fatal illness, he summoned a relative, a Benedictine abbot, and told him that he was unable to put his affairs in order and could not pay back the money earned from usury. If the relative would be accountable for his soul before God and would promise absolution from his sins, he would turn over to him all his possessions, both real and personal, to be disposed of as the abbot saw fit. The abbot saw that the man was truly contrite and repentant. He went to consult the bishop, who suggested

that the abbot answer for the usurer's soul before God and accept
his fortune, on condition that the art treasures be returned to
his cathedral church. The abbot returned in haste to the dying
man and told him what he had learned. The sick man said, "Then
my advice is that you bring carts at once, and carry out all my
property first, and take me last of all." There were two chests
of gold and silver, an infinite number of golden objects, books
and various ornaments that he had taken as collateral, a great
deal of wheat, wine, and bedding, and vast herds of animals.
When everything had been removed, the abbot had the sick
man put into a sedan chair and hastened off to the monastery.
But the sick man had barely entered the gates of the monastery
when he expired. The abbot, who had not forgotten his pledge,
returned as much of the usurious gain as he could and gave very
large alms for the usurer's soul, and turned the rest of his property over to the use of the monks. The body was placed in a
chapel, surrounded by choirs of singers. That very night, four
black spirits appeared to the brothers who were singing and
took their place to the left of the coffin. At the sight, all the
monks, except for the oldest, fled in terror. Four angels suddenly appeared and took their places to the right of the coffin,
opposite the demons. The demons chanted Psalm 36 of David,
in which God promises to punish injustice, and they said, "If
God be just and His words true, this man is ours, because he is
guilty of all these things." The holy angels replied, "If you bring
forward against him this psalm of David, go on with it.... Since
you are silent, we will bring forward the rest of the psalm."
And they sang the psalmist's lines about God's unfathomable
justice and His mercy and His promises, saying: " 'The children of men shall put their trust under the shadow of Thy
wings'.... Because God is just, and the Scripture cannot be bro-

ken, this child of man is ours; he fled to the Lord, and to the
Lord he shall go, because he put his trust under the shadow of
His wings: 'He shall be satisfied with the pleasures of His house,'
for he hath bewailed himself with the tears of contrition." Under
the noses of the dumbfounded and speechless demons, the angels
carried the soul of the contrite sinner off to Paradise, recalling
Jesus's words, "There will be joy before the angels of God over
one repentant sinner" [Luke 15:10].[8]

This story from Caesarius of Heisterbach's book, *Of Contrition*,
highlights the power of contrition. A usurer who has repented
in extremis goes straight to Paradise, without even passing through
Purgatory, although a large part of his penance was actually carried out by the abbot, whose monastery received a few crumbs
of the usurer's fortune. (Was this lawful interest?) To the novice's question, "Which was the more helpful to this usurer, his
alms or his contrition?" Caesarius replies, "If contrition had
been lacking, his alms would have profited him but little."

And so, beyond Purgatory, the thirteenth-century usurer
became caught up in the movement of Christian devotion toward
the inner life. A usurer's salvation was well worth some trouble, and one had to trust that, with or without Purgatory, God
would save usurers whom, in the absence of confession and
restitition, He alone knew had felt true contrition. But contrition is more than a few words on the tip of one's tongue. If the
usurer has a heart, that heart must speak out. To the novice's
naïve but opportune question about whether a man without eyes
can be contrite, since one cannot weep if one has no eyes,
Caesarius replies, "Contrition does not consist in tears but in
the emotion of the heart, whose outward signs are indeed tears
of the eyes, but the heart has tears of its own." And he adds,
"Every man, whether he has been righteous or a sinner, if he

dies in the very least contrition [*in contritione etiam minima*], will see God."[9]

Jacques de Vitry ends his second sermon on usurers with a hymn to the repentant usurer. "After he is converted to God, 'his name is honorable before Him.' He who formerly was called cruel shall be called merciful, he who was called fox and monkey shall be called lamb and dove, he who was called the Devil's servant shall be called the servant of Our Lord Jesus Christ who liveth...."[10]

Clearly, Purgatory was just one of the complicitous winks that Christianity sent the usurer's way during the thirteenth century, but it was the only one that gave him unrestricted assurance of Paradise. Purgatory was *hope*. Caesarius of Heisterbach points this out when discussing, not a usurer, but a woman sinner whose fate is equally as hellish. His story is of a young nun, who had fornicated with a monk, and God had caused her to die in childbirth, along with the fruit of her sin.[11]

For the usurer who was ready for final contrition, Purgatory was the hope and, soon, the quasi-certainty of being saved, of being able to have both his money, here below, *and* his life, his eternal life beyond the grave. The usurer of Liège was the symbol of hope. Thanks to usury, the usurer hoped to make material, financial profits. Thomas of Chobham, for example, observes: "If someone lends to someone else at interest, even though he may hope [*sperare*] to collect interest on the loan in return...." The lender seems disposed to prefer this earthly hope to another hope, a heavenly hope. Hope against hope. But the hope of Purgatory leads to the hope of Paradise. After a more or less lengthy stay in Purgatory, one *obligatorily* goes to Paradise. Riches and Paradise: a double hope.

One robin does not make a springtime, and a usurer in Purgatory does not mean capitalism. One economic system replaces another only after it has passed through a long and varied obstacle course. History is people, and the instigators of capitalism were usurers: merchants of the future, sellers of time, which Leon Battista Alberti would define as money in the fifteenth century. These men were Christians, but it was not the *earthly* consequences of the Church's condemnation of usury that restrained them, on the threshold of capitalism; it was the agonizing fear of Hell. In a society where all conscience was a religious conscience, obstacles were first of all — or finally — religious. The hope of escaping Hell, thanks to Purgatory, permitted the usurer to propel the economy and society of the thirteenth century ahead toward capitalism.

Post Scriptum

This essay had been completed when I came upon a corroborating passage in an excellent article by Elizabeth A. R. Brown.

> In a *quodlibet* [university exercise] written at the end of the thirteenth century, Renier de Clairmarais examined the question of knowing whether a person, whose testamentary executors deferred distributing property he had left, would therefore be forced to remain longer than otherwise in Purgatory. Renier decided that if the property had been left for purposes of restitution, delay would not affect the length of time spent in Purgatory unless the testator had knowingly selected irresponsible executors; if, however, the testator had left the property as alms to gain forgiveness for his sins, his release from Purgatory would be delayed, although his suffering would not be increased. Renier warned that executors sinned gravely in deferring distribution of such bequests; they should, he said, be compelled to act by a superior authority and should be excommunicated if they failed to take action.[12]

The usurer in Purgatory has been incorporated into the university curriculum.

Appendices

Appendix A: Dante, *The Divine Comedy*

Così ancor su per la strema testa
di quel settimo cerchio tutto solo
andai, dove sedea la gente mesta.

Per li occhi fora scoppiava lor duolo;
di qua, di là soccorrièn con le mani
quando a' vapori, et quando al caldo suolo:

non altrimenti fan di state i cani
or col ceffo or col piè, quando son morsi
o da pulci o da mosche o da tafani.

Poi che nel viso a certi li occhi porsi,
ne' quali 'l doloroso foco casca,
non ne conobbi alcun; ma io m'accorsi

che dal collo a ciascun pendea una tasca
ch'avea certo colore e certo segno,
e quindi par che 'l loro occhio si pasca.

E com' io riguardando tra lor vegno,
in una borsa gialla vidi azzurro
che d'un leone avea faccia et contegno.

Poi, procedendo di mio sguardo il curro,
vidine un'altra come sangue rossa,
mostrando un'oca bianca più che burro.

E un che d'una scrofa azzurra e grossa
segnato avea lo suo sacchetto bianco,
mi disse: "Che fai tu in questa fossa?

Or te ne va; et perchè se' vivo anco,
sappi che 'l mio vicin Vitalïano
sederà qui dal mio sinistro fianco.

Con questi fiorentin son padovano:
spesse fiate m' intronan le orecchi
gridando: Vegna il cavalier sovrano,

che recherà la tasca coi tre becchi!"
Qui distorse la bocca et di fuor trasse
la lingua, come bue che 'l naso lecchi.

Et io, temendo no 'l più star crucciasse
lui che di poco star m'avea 'mmonito,
torna' mi in dietro dall'anime lasse.

So I went by myself still farther along the extreme margin of the seventh circle, where the woeful people were seated. Their grief was bursting forth through their eyes; with their hands they defended themselves, now here, now there, sometimes from the flames, sometimes from the burning ground; not otherwise do the dogs in summer, now with muzzle, now with paw, when they are bitten by fleas, or flies, or gadflies. When I set my eyes on the faces of some of these on whom the grievous fire descends, I did not recognize any of them, but I perceived that from the neck of each hung a pouch, which had a certain color and a certain device, and thereon each seems to feast his eyes. And when I came among them, looking about, I saw, upon a yellow purse, azure that had the form and bearing of a lion. Then, gazing farther, I saw another, red as blood, display a goose whiter than butter. And one, who had his white wallet marked with an azure and gravid sow, said to me, "What are you doing in this ditch? Now get you gone! And since you are still alive, know that my neighbor Vitaliano shall sit here at my left side. With these Florentines am I, a Paduan; often they din my ears, shouting, 'Let the sovereign knight come who will bring the pouch with three goats!'" Then he twisted his mouth and stuck out his tongue, like an ox that licks its nose; and I, fearing lest a longer stay should anger him who had admonished me to stay but little, turned back from the weary souls.[1]

APPENDIX B: Ezra Pound, *Canto XLV*

With Usura

With usura hath no man a house of good stone
each block cut smooth and well-fitting
that design might cover their face,
with usura
hath no man a painted paradise on his church wall
harpes et luz
or where virgin receiveth message
and halo projects from incision,
with usura
seeth no man Gonzaga his heirs and his concubines
no picture is made to endure nor to live with
but it is made to sell and sell quickly
with usura, sin against nature,
is thy bread ever more of stale rags
is thy bread dry as paper,
with no mountain wheat, no strong flour
with usura the line grows thick
with usura no clear demarcation
and no man can find site for his dwelling.
Stonecutter is kept from his stone
weaver is kept from his loom
WITH USURA
wool comes not to market
sheep bringeth no gain with usura
Usura is a murrain, usura
blunteth the needle in the maid's hand
and stoppeth the spinner's cunning. Pietro Lombardo

came not by usura
Duccio came not by usura
nor Pier della Francesca; Zuan Bellin' not by usura
nor was 'la Calunnia' painted.
Came not by usura Angelico; came not Ambrogio Praedis,
Came no church of cut stone signed: Adamo me fecit.
Not by usura St Trophime
Not by usura Saint Hilaire,
Usura rusteth the chisel
It rusteth the craft and the craftsman
It gnaweth the thread in the loom
None learneth to weave gold in her pattern;
Azure hath a canker by usura; cramoisi is unbroidered
Emerald findeth no Memling
Usura slayeth the child in the womb
It stayeth the young man's courting
It hath brought palsey to bed, lyeth
between the young bride and her bridegroom
                    CONTRA NATURAM

They have brought whores for Eleusis
Corpses are set to banquet
at behest of usura.[2]

APPENDIX C: Ezra Pound, *Addendum for Canto C*

The Evil is Usury, neschek
the serpent
neschek *whose name is known, the defiler,*
beyond race and against race
the defiler
Τόχος; hic mali medium est
Here is the core of evil, the burning hell without let-up,
The canker corrupting all things, Fafnir the worm,
Syphilis of the State, of all kingdoms,
Wart of the commonweal,
Wenn-maker, corrupter of all things.
Darkness the defiler,
Twin evil of envy,
Snake of the seven heads, Hydra, entering all things,
Passing the doors of temples, defiling the Grove of Paphos,
neschek, *the crawling evil,*
slime, the corrupter of all things,
Poisoner of the fount,
of all fountains, neschek,
The serpent, evil against Nature's increase,
Against beauty
     Τὸ χαλόν
    formosus nec est nec decens
A thousand are dead in his folds,

         in the eel-fisher's basket
    Χαίρη! Ω Διώνη, Χαίρη
   pure Light, we beseech thee
   Crystal, we beseech thee
Clarity, we beseech thee.[3]

I wish to thank Jacques Berlioz for having called my attention to these magnificent and revealing poems about the medieval phenomenon of usury. On Ezra Pound's economic ideas, one must read the chapter entitled "Poundwise: Towards a General Critique of Economy," in Jean-Michel Rabaté's remarkable study, *Language, Sexuality and Ideology in Ezra Pound's Cantos* (London: MacMillan, 1986), pp. 183–241. I am especially grateful to Mr. Rabaté for having made these pages available to me before his book became available in France.

Notes

CHAPTER I

1. As money is called in Gautier de Châtillon's goliard poems of the late twelfth century.

2. As it was said of Christ, in royal liturgy and on the gold *écus* minted under Louis IX.

3. The sermon "*Ad status*," number 58,17.

CHAPTER II

1. Ezra Pound, *The Cantos*, see Appendix B.

2. Thomas of Chobham, *Summa confessorum*, ed. F. Broomfield (Louvain, 1986), question XI, chapter I, p. 504.

3. K. Polanyi and C. Arensberg, *Trade and Market in the Early Empires* (Glencoe, 1957), p. 74.

4. *Ibid.*, p. 242.

5. *Dictionnaire de théologie catholique* (Paris, 1950), s.v. "Usure," by G. Le Bras, col. 2356.

6. Robert of Courçon, "Le traité 'De usura' de Robert de Courçon," ed. G. Lefèvre, *Travaux et mémoires de l'université de Lille* 10 (1902): 35.

7. William of Auxerre, *Summa in IV libros sententiarum*, book III, tr. xxvi.

8. Especially in his *Summa theologica*, II[a], II[ae], q. 78.

9. *Breviarium in ps LIV*, *Patrologia latina*, tome XVI, col. 982.

10. Commentary on Ezek. 18:6, *Patrologia latina*, tome XXV, col. 117.

11. Gratian, *Decretum*, C. 14, q. 3, c. 4.

12. Thomas of Chobham, *Summa confessorum*, p. 504.

13. William of Auxerre, *Summa*, book III, tr. xxvi.

14. Thomas of Chobham, *Summa confessorum*, p. 504.

15. Stephen of Bourbon, *Anecdotes historiques, légendes et apologues tirés du recueil d'Etienne de Bourbon, dominicain du XIIIe siècle*, ed. A. Lecoy de la Marche (Paris, 1877), pp. 361-62.

16. *Patrologia latina*, tome CLVIII, col. 659.

17. *Summa theologica*, II[a], II[ae], q. 78, 20.

18. J. Ibanès, *La Doctrine de l'Eglise et les réalités économiques au XIIIe siècle: l'intérêt, les prix et la monnaie* (Paris, 1967), pp. 20-22.

19. *Summa theologica*, II[a], II[ae], q. 78, art. 1, Ibanès, *op. cit.*, *Doctrine*, p. 19.

20. St. Bonaventure, *In Tertium Sententiarum*, dist. XXXVII, dub. vii, Ibanès, *op. cit.*, *Doctrine*, p. 19.

21. Thomas of Chobham, *Summa confessorum*, p. 515.

22. II, viii in Caesarius of Heisterbach, *Caesarii Heisterbacensis...Dialogus miraculorum*. ed. J. Strange (Cologne, Bonn, Brussels, 1851), 1:73; English trans. by H. von E. Scott and C.C. Swinton Bland, *The Dialogue on Miracles* (London, 1929), 1:79-80.

23. J. Th. Welter, ed., *Tabula exemplorum secundum ordinem Alphabeti* (Paris and Toulouse, 1926), p. 83, no. 306.

24. Dante Alighieri, *The Divine Comedy*, ed. and trans. by C.S. Singleton (Princeton, 1970), vol. 1: *The Inferno*, canto XI, lines 109-11.

25. Ezra Pound, *The Cantos*, Canto XLV.

CHAPTER III

1. *Orcival*, Zodiaque editions, La Carte du Ciel, no. 11 (s.l., 1963), p. 15.

2. Stephen of Bourbon, *Anecdotes historiques*, p. 254.

3. Jacques de Vitry, *The "Exempla" or Illustrative Stories from the "Sermones vulgares" of Jacques de Vitry*, ed. T.F. Crane (London, 1890, reprint 1967), p. 72.

4. Welter, ed., *Tabula exemplorum*, p. 83.

5. Dante, *Inferno*, canto XVII, lines 54-57.

6. A. Pézard, *Dante sous la pluie de feu* (Paris, 1950), p. 101, n. 5.

7. H. Wolter and H. Holstein, gen. eds., *Histoire des Conciles oecuméniques*, 12 vols. (Paris, 1963-), vol. 6: *Latran IV*, by R. Foreville.

8. Sermon *"ad status,"* no. 58, 14.

9. Stephen of Bourbon, *Anecdotes historiques*, p. 362.

10. This Christian usurer was called *usurarius* in Latin, the language of most of the documents used for this book. This is a scholarly word borrowed from the classical Latin of antiquity and from Roman law, which uses the term *fenerator*, "he who lends at interest," derived from *fenus*, "interest," which is close to the word *fetus*, "the fruit of fertilization." But, in the case of *fenus*, is the product legitimate?

11. Thomas of Chobham, *Summa confessorum*, p. 509.

12. *Ibid.*, p. 505.

13. Welter, ed., *Tabula exemplorum*, p. 139, n. 304.

14. Thomas of Chobham, *Summa confessorum*, p. 505.

15. Bibliothèque national, Ms. Latin 13472, fol. 3vb; Welter, ed., *Tabula exemplorum*, p. 139, n. 304.

16. Thomas of Chobham, *Summa confessorum*, p. 505.

17. Robert of Courçon, *"De usura,"* p. 35.

18. *Dictionnaire de Théologie catholique*, "Usure," col. 2351.

19. Thomas of Chobham, *Summa confessorum*, p. 505.

20. Caesarius of Heisterbach, *Dialogus miraculorum*, 1:73; and *Dialogue on Miracles*, 1:80.

21. Stephen of Bourbon, *Anecdotes historiques*, pp. 334-35.

22. Welter, ed., *Tabula exemplorum*, p. 51.

23. Jean Sire de Joinville, *The Life of St. Louis*, trans. R. Hague (New York, 1955), p. 30, par. 33, which uses as its source *L'Histoire de Saint Louis*, ed. and trans. by M. Natalis de Wailly (Paris, 1874).

CHAPTER IV

1. See J. Le Goff, "Métiers licites et métiers illicites dans l'Occident médiéval," *Annales de l'Ecole des hautes études de Gand*, 5:41-57; reused in J. Le Goff, *Pour un autre Moyen Age* (Paris, 1977), pp. 91-107.

2. Thomas of Chobham, *Summa confessorum*, p. 516.

3. *Summa theologica*, II^a, II^{ae}, q. 78.

4. Thomas of Chobham, *Summa confessorum*, p. 510.

5. Caesarius of Heisterbach, II, viii, *Dialogus miraculorum*, 1:73; and *Dialogue on Miracles*, 1:80.

6. Thomas of Chobham, *Summa confessorum*, p. 509.

7. Dante, *Inferno*, canto XI, lines 49-51.

8. Welter, ed., *Tabula exemplorum*, p. 83.

9. Jacques de Vitry, *Exempla*, p. 76.

10. Sermon *"ad status"*, no. 59, 15.

11. Welter, ed., *Tabula exemplorum*, p. 76.

12. Sermon *"ad status,"* no. 59, 9.

13. Jacques de Vitry, *Exempla*, p. 73.

14. *Ibid.*, p. 74.

15. Sermon *"ad status,"* no. 59, 17.

16. R. de Roover, *La Pensée économique des scolastiques, doctrines et méthodes* (Paris, Montreal, 1971); and *Business, Banking and Economic Thought in Late Medieval and Modern Europe, Selected Studies* (Chicago, 1974).

17. J.T. Noonan, *The Scholastic Analysis of Usury* (Cambridge, Mass., 1957), p. 192.

18. Sermon *"ad status,"* no. 59, 14.

19. Welter, *Tabula exemplorum*, pp. 22-23.

20. Sermon *"ad status,"* no. 59, 15.

21. Stephen of Bourbon, *Anecdotes historiques*, pp. 365-66.

22. *Ibid.*, pp. 364-65.

23. *Ibid.*, pp. 263-64.

24. Caesarius of Heisterbach, II, vii, *Dialogus miraculorum*, 1:70-72; and *Dialogue on Miracles*, 1:76-78.

25. Stephen of Bourbon, *Anecdotes historiques*, pp. 367-68.

26. *Ibid.*, p. 368.

27. Jacques de Vitry, *Exempla*, p. 75.

28. Welter, ed., *Tabula exemplorum*, p. 83.

CHAPTER V

1. G. Nahon, "Le crédit et les Juifs dans la France du XIIIe siècle," *Annales E.S.C.* 24 (1969): 1137.

2. Caesarius of Heisterbach, XII, xxiv, *Dialogus miraculorum*, 2:335-36; and *Dialogue on Miracles*, 2:313-14.

3. *Ibid.*, XII, xviii, *Dialogus miraculorum*, 2:328; and *Dialogue on Miracles*, 2:305.

4. Stephen of Bourbon, *Anecdotes historiques*, p. 362.

5. Thomas of Chobham, *Summa confessorum*, pp. 506-07.

6. *Ibid.*, pp. 515-16.

CHAPTER VI

1. Stephen of Bourbon, *Anecdotes historiques*, p. 364.

2. Caesarius of Heisterbach, II, vii, *Dialogus miraculorum*, 1:72; and *Dialogue on Miracles*, 1:78.

3. *Ibid.*, II, vii, *Dialogus miraculorum*, 1:27; and *Dialogue on Miracles*, 1:78-79.

4. Stephen of Bourbon, *Anecdotes historiques*, p. 369.

5. *Ibid.*, pp. 366-67.

6. Caesarius of Heisterbach, III, lii, *Dialogus miraculorum*, 1:169; and *Dialogue on Miracles*, 1:190-91.

7. *Ibid.*, II, viii, *Dialogus miraculorum*, 1:73; and *Dialogue on Miracles*, 1:80.

8. *Ibid.*, II, xxxi, *Dialogus miraculorum*, 1:103-05; and *Dialogue on Miracles*, 1:116-18.

9. *Ibid.*, II, xxxiv-xxxv, *Dialogus miraculorum*, 1:108-09; and *Dialogue on Miracles*, 1:121-22.

10. Sermon, *"ad status,"* 59, 18.

11. Caesarius of Heisterbach, *Dialogus miraculorum*, XII, xxvi, 2:338; and *Dialogue on Miracles*, 2:316.

12. E.A.R. Brown, "Royal Salvation and Needs of State in Late Capetian France," in *Order and Innovation in the Middle Ages*, ed. W.C. Jordan, B. McNabb and T.F. Ruiz (Princeton, 1976), pp. 542-43, n. 14.

Appendices

1. Dante, *Inferno*, canto XVII, lines 43-78, pp. 174-77.
2. Ezra Pound, *The Cantos*, "Canto XLV."
3. *Ibid.*, "Addendum for C."

Bibliography

A. PRIMARY SOURCES

(a) Acts of Church Councils:

Leonardi, C., ed. *Conciliorum œcumenicorum decreta.* Bologna and Vienna, 1962.

Wolter, H. and H. Holstein, gen. eds. *Histoire des Conciles œcuméniques.* 12 vols. Paris. Vol. 6: *Latran I, II, III et Latran IV*, by R. Foreville, 1965; Vol. 6: *Lyon I et Lyon II*, by G. Dumeige, 1966; Vol. 8: *Vienne*, by J. Leclerc, 1964.

(b) Royal Ordinances (France):

Laurière, E. de, ed. *Ordonnances des roys de France.* Vol. 1. Paris, 1732.

(c) Confessors' Handbooks:

Astesanus, O.F.M. *Summa astesana.* Bk. III, tit. xi.

Johannes von Freibourg, O.P. *Summa confessorum.* Bk. II, tit. vii., fols. 84–91. Edited by Jean Petit, late fifteenth century.

Raymond of Peñafort, O.P. *Summa de pœnitentia.* Bk. II, tit. vii, pp. 325–45. Avignon, 1715.

Thomas of Chobham. *Summa confessorum.* Edited by F. Broomfield. Louvain, 1968.

(d) Theological Treatises:

Aquinas, Thomas. Opus LXXIII of the Roman edition of the *Works.* Edited as *De usuris* by Gilles de Lessines.

Robert of Courçon. "Le traité *De usura* de Robert de Courçon." Edited by G. Lefèvre. *Travaux et mémoires de l'université de Lille* 10 (1902), no. 30.

Van Roey, J. *De Justo auctario ex contractu crediti.* Louvain, 1903. On Thomas Aquinas and usury, see pp. 154–75.

William of Auxerre [Guillaume d'Auxerre, or Guillermus Altissiodorensis]. *Summa in IV libros sententiarum.* Bk. III, tr. xxvi.

(e) Dante:

Dante Alighieri. *The Divine Comedy.* Edited and translated by Ch. S. Singleton. 2 vols. Vol. 1: *Inferno.* Princeton, 1970.

Pézard, A. *Dante sous la pluie de feu.* Paris, 1950.

(f) Exempla:

Brémond, Cl., J. Le Goff, and J. Cl. Schmitt. *L'"Exemplum."* Typologie des Sources du Moyen Age occidental, fasc. 40. Turnhout, 1982.

Caesarius of Heisterbach. *Caesarii Heisterbacensis...Dialogus miraculorum.* Edited by J. Strange. 2 vols. Cologne, Bonn and Brussels, 1851.

———— *The Dialogue on Miracles.* Translated by H. von E. Scott and C.C. Swinton Bland. 2 vols. London, 1929.

Jacques de Vitry [Jacobus de Vitriaco]. *The "Exempla" or Illustrative Stories from the "Sermones vulgares" of Jacques de Vitry.* Edited by T.F. Crane. London, 1890, reprinted 1967.

———— *Exempla* transcribed from manuscript sources by Marie-Claire Gasnault, whom I wish to thank.

Schmitt, J. Cl., ed. *Prêcher d'exemples, Récit de prédicateurs du Moyen Age.* Paris, 1985.

Stephen of Bourbon [Etienne de Bourbon, or Stephanus de Borbone]. *Anecdotes historiques, légendes et apologues tirés du recueil inédit d'Etienne de Bourbon, dominicain du XIIIe siècle.* Edited by A. Lecoy de la Marche. Paris, 1877.

———— *Exempla* transcribed from manuscript sources by Jacques Berlioz, whom I wish to thank.

Welter, J.Th., ed. La *"Tabula exemplorum secundum ordinem alphabeti."* Paris and Toulouse, 1926. A collection of *exempla* compiled at the end of the thirteenth century.

B. SECONDARY WORKS ON USURY AND THE USURER

Baldwin, J.W. *The Medieval Theories of the Just Price. Romanists, Canonists and Theologians in the Twelfth and Thirteenth Centuries.* Transactions of the American Philosophical Society, N.S., vol. 49, Philadelphia, 1959.

Capitani, O. "Il *De peccato usure* di Remigio de' Girolami." In *Per la storia della cultura in Italia nel Duecento e primo Trecento.* Omaggio a Dante nel VII Centenario della Nuscita, Spoleto, 1965. Special issue of *Studi Medievali,* ser. 3, a. VI, fasc. II (1965): 537–662.

_____ ed. *L'Etica economica medievale.* Bologna, 1974.

de Roover, R. *La pensée économique des scolastiques, doctrines et methodes.* Paris and Montreal, 1971.

Dictionnaire de théologie catholique. Paris, 1950. S.v. "Usure," XV, col. 2336–2372. Article by G. Le Bras.

Helmholz, R.H. "Usury and the Medieval English Church Courts." In *Speculum,* Vol. 6, no. 2 (1986): 364–80.

Ibanès, J. *La Doctrine de l'Eglise et les réalités économiques au XIIIe siècle: l'intérêt, les prix et la monnaie.* Paris, 1967.

Kirschner, J. and K. Lo Prete. "Peter John Olivi's Treatises on Contracts of Sale, Usury and Restitution: Minority Economics or Minor Works?" *Quaderni fiorentini* 13 (1984): 233–86.

Le Goff, J. *Marchands et banquiers au Moyen Age.* Paris, 1956, and 6th ed., 1980.

_____ "Usure et à peu près." In *Mélanges offerts à Georges Guilbaud.* (Forthcoming.)

_____ "The Usurer and Purgatory." In *The Dawn of Modern Banking,* pp. 25–52. Center for Medieval and Renaissance Studies, University of California. Los Angeles, 1979.

Luzzatto, G. "Tasso d'interesse e usura a Venezia nei secoli XIII–XV." In *Miscellanea in onore di Roberto Cessi* 1: 191–202. Rome, 1958.

McLaughlin, T.P. "The Teaching of the Canonists on Usury (Twelfth, Thirteenth and Fourteenth Centuries)." *Medieval Studies* 1 (1939): 82–107; and 2 (1940): 1–22.

Nahon, G. "Le crédit et les Juifs dans la France du XIIIe siècle." *Annales E.S.C.* 24 (1969): 1121–48.

Nelson, B.N. *The Idea of Usury: From Tribal Brotherhood to Universal Otherhood.* Princeton, 1949; 2nd ed. Chicago, 1969.

———— "The Usurer and the Merchant Prince: Italian Businessmen and the Ecclesiastical Law of Restitution, 1100–1500." *Journal of Economic History*, supplement 7 (1947): 104–122.

Noonan, J.T. *The Scholastic Analysis of Usury.* Cambridge, Mass., 1957.

Salvioli, G. "La dottrina dell 'usura secondi i canonisti et i civilisti italiani dei secoli XII e XIV." *Studi Fadda* 3 (1906): 259–78.

Sapori, A. "L'interesse del danaro a Firenze nel Trecento." *Archivo Storico Italiano* (1928): 161–86.

———— "L'usura nel Dugento a Pistoia." *Studi mediœvali* II (1929): 208–16.

Schilperoort, G. *Le Commerçant dans la littérature française du Moyen Age.* Groningen, 1933.

Schnapper, B. "La répression de l'usure et l'évolution économique." *Tijdschrift voor Rechtsgeschiedenis* 37 (1969): 53–57.

C. Secondary Works Shedding Light on Usury and the Medieval Usurer

Ariès, P. "Richesse et pauvreté devant la mort." In *Etudes sur l'histoire de la pauvreté (Moyen Age–XVIe siècle)* 2:519–33. Edited by M. Mollat. Paris, 1974.

Baldwin, J.W. *Masters, Princes and Merchants: The Social Views of Peter the Chanter and His Circle.* 2 vols. Princeton, 1970.

Beriou, N. "Autour de Latran IV (1215): la naissance de la confession moderne et sa diffusion." In Groupe de la Buissière, *Pratiques de la confession*, pp. 73–93. Paris, 1983.

Brown, E.A.R. "Royal Salvation and Needs of State in Late Capetian France." In *Order and Innovation in the Middle Ages. Essays in Honor of Joseph R. Strayer*, pp. 365–83, 541–61. Edited by W.C. Jordan, B. McNabb, and T.F. Ruiz. Princeton, 1976.

Chenu, M.D. *L'Eveil de la conscience dans la civilisation médiévale*. Montréal-Paris, 1969.

de Roover, R. *Business, Banking and Economic Thought in Late Medieval and Modern Europe: Selected Studies*. Edited by J. Kirschner. Chicago, 1974.

Gilchrist, J. *The Church and Economic Activity in the Middle Ages*. New York, 1969.

Le Goff, J. *Les intellectuels au Moyen Age*. Paris, 1957; new ed. 1985.

————— "Métier et profession d'après les manuels de confesseurs du Moyen Age." In *Miscellanea Mediaevalia, Beiträge zum Berufsbewustsein des mittelalterlichen Menschen*, Vol. III, pp. 44–60. Berlin, 1964. Reprinted in J. Le Goff, *Pour un autre Moyen Age*, pp. 162–80. Paris, 1977.

————— "Métiers licites et métiers illicites dans l'Occident médiéval." *Annales de l'Ecole des hautes études de Gand*, vol. 5, pp. 41–57. Reprinted in J. Le Goff, *Pour un autre Moyen Age*. Paris, 1977.

————— *La Naissance du Purgatoire*. Paris, 1981.

Little, L.K. "Pride Goes before Avarice: Social Change and the Vices in Latin Christendom." *American Historical Review* 76 (1971): 16–49.

————— *Religious Poverty and the Profit Economy in Medieval Europe*. London, 1978.

Lopez, R.S. *The Commercial Revolution of the Middle Ages, 950–1350*. Englewood Cliffs, N.J., 1971.

Murray, A. *Reason and Society in the Middle Ages*. Oxford, 1978.

Parkes, J.W. *The Jew in the Medieval Community: A Study of His Political and Economic Situation*. London, 1938.

Pirenne, H. *Histoire économique et sociale du Moyen Age*. New ed. Paris, 1969.

Polanyi, K., and C. Arensberg. *Trade and Market in the Early Empires.* Glencoe, 1957.

Tractenberg, J. *The Devil and the Jews: The Medieval Conception of the Jew and Its Relations to Modern Anti-Semitism.* New Haven, 1943.

This edition designed by Bruce Mau
Type composed by Archie at Canadian Composition